On the Edge

On the Edge

Religious Freedom and Persecution Across Asia

Michael Kelly SJ

UCAN ·))》

2016

Title: On the edge : religious freedom and persecution across Asia / edited by Michael Kelly.

ISBN: 9781925371109 (paperback)
        9781925371116 (hardback)
        9781925371123 (ebook : epub)
        9781925371130 (ebook : Kindle)
        9781925371147 (ebook : pdf)

Subjects: Freedom of religion--Asia. Persecution--Asia. Other Creators/ Contributors: Kelly, Michael 1953 January 16- editor.
Dewey Number: 261.72

Layout by UCAN and Astrid Sengkey
Cover design by Astrid Sengkey.

Text Minion Pro Size 10 &11

Published by:

An imprint of the ATF Press
Publishing Group owned by ATF (Australia) Ltd.
PO Box 504
Hindmarsh, SA 5007
ABN 90 116 359 963
www.atfpress.com
Making a lasting impact

Table of Contents

Introduction

Jesus warned his followers to expect persecution, and he spoke from experience: 'If the world hates you, know that it has hated me before it hated you' (John 15:18). And he gave advice on what to do about it: 'Love your enemies and pray for those who persecute you' (Matthew 5:44).

Today, Christians have plenty of enemies, especially in certain parts of Asia.

But Asia, as a geographic entity, is a European invention. It stretches from the eastern shores of the Mediterranean to the east coast of the Philippines. Asia Minor—referring to what is now called the Middle East—was no less a European designation. But east of where? Europe.

Asia's north-south boundaries are also vast—extending from the Torres Strait—the expanse of water south of Indonesia's eastern province of Irian Jaya—to the Russian arctic.

However it is viewed—geographically, politically, historically or culturally—the continent takes in more people, cultures, languages, religions, political ideologies and economic arrangements than any other continent on earth. And with the rate of economic development in the region outstripping the rest of the world, the 21st century is often described as being the 'Asian century.' And so it will be for Christianity.

Any attempt to refer to the continent in a unified way, as if it were in any way a coherent entity, does not help in understanding what life is actually like in disparate Asian societies. What do Sri Lankans and Koreans have in common apart from being called Asians? What common cultural traits do Nepalis and Timorese share? About as much as Chinese and Indians, which is not a great deal.

Asia is the home of some of the world's great religious traditions. Buddhism, Hinduism and the various religious and ethnic traditions of China—Daoism and Confucianism—were all born here. And if the old definition of Asia that included the Middle East applies, we can add Judaism, Islam and Christianity. Indeed, Asia is the source from which all of the world's great religions have sprung.

With its religious, cultural, political and economic diversity, it is no surprise that the contours and shapes of religious persecution in Asia also vary greatly –from outright and violent suppression, to systematic exclusion from opportunities in work and public life, to unstated prejudices that create negative personal judgments. All of these occur in one or other Asian country—sometimes several of them together. Apart from the Philippines and Timor-Leste, where Christians are in the majority, most Asian Christians are in minority groups, often with few resources to protect themselves when prejudice turns to persecution.

Persecution in Asian societies has a history tied to each particular nationality. Christianity's first record in Asia is still visible in China today. Christians first appeared in the western Chinese city of Xian in 635, capital of the Tang Dynasty (618–907 AD), and their creed is enscribed in surviving tablets. They were Nestorians, who came to Asia when their leader Nestorius was condemned as a heretic at the Council of Ephesus (431 AD). Nestorius (386–450 AD) was the patriarch of Constantinople (today's Istanbul), and after his removal from that post, his followers fled further and further east until they arrived in China.

But, as happened three more times in Chinese history, that Christian period came to an end with persecution by the imperial authorities in the late 10th century.

Christianity's most expansive period in Asia began with the arrival of European merchants from the 15th century on wards. Along with the traders came the missionaries—to India, China, Japan, Indonesia, Thailand and the Malay Peninsula. Portuguese, Spanish, French, Dutch and English traders were among the earliest. And they all brought their chaplains. Their monarchs, administrators, entrepreneurs and armies saw their mission as not just to develop commercial opportunities but also to bring the message of Jesus Christ to those they feared would be banished from God's sight without baptism.

The spread of the Gospel gained impetus during the most vigorous era of European colonialist expansion in the 18th and 19th centuries. With the resources available to them, colonial armies and administrators protected Christians, and persecution of Christians declined, with the notable exceptions of Korea, Japan and Vietnam, where martyrdom was the fate of many well into the 19th century.

However, with the end of colonialism during the 20th century, Christian churches became localised in Asian cultures and settings. With that development came significant consequences for them.

Persecution across Asia

The reality of Christian persecution across Asia—today and throughout history—provides an expansive panorama from insistent discrimination that excludes Christians from opportunities in work, education, health and human development to systematic, ruthless and violent treatment that creates martyrs for the faith across denominations.

The panorama of experience is so large that only a few instances can be given within the limits of this presentation, to offer some appreciation of the nature of persecution in a continent that is rich in religious traditions but also in the abusive mistreatment of believers who do not conform to local norms. Two countries that highlight some features in a varied context are China and Pakistan.

China

Persecution comes in all shapes and sizes in China, and has done for a long time. It has ranged from full scale, murderous pogroms against Christians and other religious groups, to the slow water torture perfected by the Chinese as a method of extracting information and forcing compliance. It still has its variants, even if today's practitioners don't use water and are very adept in cyberspace.

No publically identified Christian or member of any religious association is allowed any space to act independently. Every word and action is closely watched. As Bishop Louis Jin, who died in 2013, was fond of saying: 'Nothing can happen in China without two groups knowing—the Holy Trinity and the Communist Party.' For this reason he favored complete openness. Any attempt at secrecy would always be undone.

Today, China's administrative bureaucracy overseeing the 'orderly conduct of life' is double the size it was 20 years ago. Following the predictable but profoundly disturbing (to the Communist Party) calls for democracy in Tiananmen Square in 1989, the number of people supervising the Chinese public has risen from 20 million to 40 million. And just before Easter 2014, China's President Xi Jinping chaired the first meeting of a new committee with plenipotentiary powers to maintain internal and external security, reporting not through government channels but directly to him and the small Cabinet in the Politburo.

This committee allows the president to exercise unprecedented, direct power over all aspects of the internal life and external relations of China. He has as much influence through this and other means as the creator of contemporary China, Deng Xiaoping. And he now appears to have levers of power over people to an extent matched only by the founder of modern China, Mao Zedong.

These constraints feed into an already well-controlled environment. Even in a would-be cosmopolitan metropolis like Shanghai, Party controls range from the house arrest of the local bishop to ordinary local Catholics being prevented from attending international Catholic meetings because they have a record at the local Religious Affairs Bureau. Every move is noted and reported, and passports are granted or withdrawn depending on 'acceptable' behavior.

These efforts are a bit like the boy with his finger in the dyke trying to prevent the deluge: how long can the apparatus of surveillance, constraint and control be maintained?

Signs abound that the creaking system is straining to hold together. For instance, thousands of Christians in eastern China rallied in early 2014 to protect their churches from invasion and destruction by government officials concerned that Christianity is growing too fast and in an 'unsustainable' way in China. In one case, a community camped out overnight to protect its church, fearing that if they did not keep watch, the bulldozers would move in under cover of darkness.

Protestant communities in Beijing especially—both authorised and 'underground'—are constant targets of scrutiny. The Chinese government routinely suppresses information about unregistered Protestant communities, and in 2011 forced onto the streets the Shouwang Church, an influential underground church in Beijing.

The government of China has good reason to fear the unregulated Christian communities in Beijing. They are also associated with movements for the introduction of multi-party democracy. It has been claimed by many commentators that Christianity represents the largest social movement in the country today, even with suggestions that China will have the world's largest population of Protestant Christians by 2030.

But the social movement is far from coherent in its strategies and approaches. In northern China, Protestant communities are almost all advocates of democratic reform. In southern China, an alternative is preferred—the creation of space for believers to gather, celebrate their faith and enlarge their membership through the creation and use of institutions in civil society that have no direct political purpose.

This restiveness among Christians reflects something broader in China. Throughout the country, popular dissatisfaction with how China is being run has escalated rapidly, to the point where even official figures reported by public security officials registered over 128,000 instances of mass unrest in 2012, up from a few thousand in the mid-1990s. An 'event of unrest' qualifies for reporting when it involves more than30 people.

To address the recurrent complaints of its citizens, Beijing has instituted a form of petitioning under which aggrieved citizens can make formal complaints. Yet that approach recently became problematic in Henan Province, when local officials blocked the way for petitioners who sought entry to a hotel where those receiving the petitions were installed.

In reality, what has always applied in China still does—Beijing is a long way from everywhere, and what is promulgated in the capital may have no purchase when it comes down to a local official's opportunity to ignore or countermand it.

The history of persecution of Christians has, on two occasions, seen the disappearance of believers—the violent suppression of the Nestorian Christians, and the flight of any survivors in the 10th and

11th centuries, and the suppression and expulsion of missionaries by imperial direction (along with the suppression of the Jesuits by the Portuguese and eventually the pope) during the 18th century.

Christian missionaries returned (along with the arrival of European traders) from the 1840s, when the Chinese emperor was forced to grant trading and occupation 'concessions' in the notorious 'unequal treaties' of that time.

This record once prompted Bishop Jin of Shanghai to explain his strategy of accepting that the Communists ran the government of China, leading to others to attack him for cooperation with the Party. The late bishop said he adopted his approach after 27 years of various forms of imprisonment (1955–1982) because, 'Christianity has had three starts in China. I don't want it to have to have a fourth.'

But shortly before his death, Bishop Jin witnessed his chosen successor making a move that set back the new bishop's and everyone else's plan: Bishop Ma announced after his Episcopal ordination that he would be resigning from his post in the government-sponsored Chinese Catholic Patriotic Association (CCPA) to concentrate on his pastoral job as bishop.

That would not be if the Religious Affairs Bureau had anything to say about it. The new bishop was stripped of his authorisation by the government, and has been under house arrest ever since, accessible to only a few people and lodged in the Shanghai seminary building that was closed as punishment at the same time, with the seminarians sent to their home dioceses or other seminaries.

As an already divided group—between those who share in the life of the officially recognised and publically operating diocese of Shanghai, and those who believe the only good Catholic is the one who makes no concessions to the government—Shanghai Catholics have had to deal with a new conundrum: a Vatican- and government-approved bishop not allowed to operate by the government.

Shanghai has only one resident bishop, with a Vatican-appointed 'underground' bishop having died in early 2014. Over recent months, relations between the Vatican and Beijing seem to have softened, leading some to speculate that the government, as a gesture of goodwill, may rehabilitate Bishop Ma.

Ma is now actually an admired figure among most Catholics from both communities in Shanghai because of his decision to split from the CCPA, and the subsequent treatment he has endured in confinement.

The supreme irony is that the government's heavy-handed treatment of Bishop Ma may be the catalyst that helps create the long-sought figure for unifying Catholics in Shanghai.

Pakistan

One way of appreciating what is happening to Christians in Pakistan —where they are a small, mostly uneducated and impoverished group —is to examine the international fallout created by their persecution, and trace that back to its source.

Thailand's capital, Bangkok, has reached a breaking point in its capacity to handle the rush of refugees and asylum seekers from Pakistan. There are approaching 8,000 asylum seekers in Bangkok, with a flow from late 2013 that is unlikely to decline as the swirl of violence increases in many parts of a country in which a corrupt government is said to control no more than a third of the total area.

A significant majority of the asylum seekers coming on tourist visas to Thailand and seeking refuge are Pakistani Christians, according to agency workers dealing with the arrivals. In 2015, asylum seekers from Syria have joined them.

The escapees from Pakistan report being persecuted by Islamic militants licensed to do what they like to 'infidels.'

Local Thai agencies—secular NGOs and Church-based agencies —are overwhelmed as they seek to provide food, accommodation, education for the children, medical care for the sick, and jobs where they can be found.

Asylum seekers coming from Pakistan get a sympathetic hearing from the United Nations High Commission for Refugees (UNHCR) because its officers know what Pakistani Christians and members of Muslim minorities are subject to in their homeland.

But the UNHCR's resources are stretched to the limit. With excessive demand on the UN agency in meeting the challenge posed by the civil war in Syria, there is little left for meeting the requirements in Thailand. Since October 2013, the waiting times for would-be refugees to have their cases for refugee status heard have blown out from 18 months from their date of arrival in Bangkok to now waiting three and a half to four years to get their story and status assessed.

Meanwhile, Pakistan continues to generate asylum seekers fearful that what happened during Holy Week, 2014, could be their lot. On the Wednesday of Holy Week (April 16), a 22-year-old janitor, a Christian living in Lahore, was shot in the head by a Muslim security guard colleague when the Christian refused to convert to Islam.

Haroon, also known as Sunny, had recently been employed, and his assailant, Umer Farooq, had been pressuring him to convert to Islam, which Haroon declined. For his refusal, he was shot dead.

Routine abuse, casual beatings in the workplace or in social venues, and regular murders are the lot of Christians in Pakistan, according to Simon, an asylum seeker from Karachi currently in Bangkok.

'Christians are taunted with being told 'you are Christians, you are not patriotic Pakistanis because in fact you belong to the Americans, the British or Gora people who kill our Muslim brothers and sisters', Simon said.

The heart of the problem for Pakistani Christians are the notorious blasphemy laws, introduced in 1988 by the assassinated president and military strongman, General Zia ul Haq. Under these blasphemy laws, a Muslim assailant can simply claim that someone has insulted the Prophet, presenting no supporting testimony or evidence other than the accusation, and the assailant is said to be entitled to execute the offending 'infidel.' What is worse, the police and courts in Pakistan are prevented from charging anyone who claims that let hal violence was motivated by the Muslim faith, and so they cannot be brought to justice.

'Where can we Pakistani Christians go in this world?' Simon asks.'We are Christians to Muslims states, so we are not welcome there. We are Pakistanis to other countries, and not welcome in them either. Where do we find a home?'

Patterns of persecution in Asia

The way Christians are treated is a product of forces and policies that apply more broadly than to Christians only. It is a product of whatever minority policy prevails, and of the often historically founded approach to minorities that applies in specific countries.

That said, the panorama of Christian communities across Asia does not present a coherent picture to the outside observer—and the persecution of Christians is varied across Asian countries, and is difficult to generalise about, except within national boundaries.

Some countries in Asia are either diverse in their religious makeup —religiously pluralist such as Malaysia, Myanmar and even India, which, remarkably, is home to more Muslims within its boundaries than its Muslim majority neighbor, Pakistan—while others are noted for divisions among the religion that predominates, such as the divisions in Islam that are evident in Pakistan, Bangladesh and Indonesia, or in China, for example, where Protestant Christianity is growing much faster than Catholicism, and the strategies and dispositions of different Protestant communities present a far from clear picture.

The different contexts in each country have consequences for Christians and the persecutions that many endure. Moreover, the treatment of Christians is usually affected by larger and broader economic, tribal, ethnic and political factors.

In some countries—China, Myanmar, Indonesia and Sri Lanka, for example—governments manage religions under the rubric of 'minority policies.' Each of those countries has significant(in China, in the tens of millions of citizens), but actually relatively small, Christian minorities – Indonesia's Christian population, for example, accounts for about 5 percent of the national population.

The rights of Christians may be supported constitutionally, as in Indonesia, but overall treatment of Christians by government agencies—the police and security forces, in the main – has Christians lumped together with other ethnic, religious or tribal groups. Often, the persecution they may experience comes as a result of national government policies and approaches that are not directed at Christians as such, but because they belong to a particular minority, ethnic or tribal group. This happens, for example, in Myanmar, where significant tribal groupings—the Karen and Chin people, in particular—have substantial Christian populations within them. Christians may be among those targeted by government, but often only because of the ethnic origin—which poses a threat to central government controls.

In Sri Lanka, Tamil Christians endure hardships because they are Tamils. Karen Christians in Myanmar get caught in conflicts with police and the military because of the independence they seek, rather than the Christian faith that many of them declare and practice. As well, in Myanmar, the targets for militant Buddhists are more Muslims than Christians, though the latter can get swept up in conflicts that are the result of perceived threats to the coherence of a 'national Buddhist culture.'

Christians in Pakistan are the victims of a failed state's inability to govern two-thirds of its territory, allowing militant and fanatical Muslims to kill Christians as a duty they claim to have because Christians are 'infidels' who should die if they won't convert to Islam.

Regional factors within large countries have their part to play in explaining how Christians fare. In India, a growing Christian population receives varied treatment depending on how local Hindus act in different parts of the subcontinent.

India's borders, as they exist today, is a product of British colonialism. Today's country was previously a territory where control was broken up into principalities led by maharajas, nawabs and other local and regional aristocrats. The subcontinent became unified under British imperial rule only after the Indian Mutiny (1857), and remained that way for 90 years until independence was achieved in 1948, and Pakistan and India were separated.

But the Indo-Pakistan break-up was done to give minority Muslims a national stronghold in Pakistan. This development reflected only the most obvious divide along religions lines in India. Remarkable for its national unity despite the immense religious diversity, India can still see conflicts caused by disputes in which one religious group persecutes another.

Asia is home to three of the four surviving communist governments in the world, and perhaps the best-resourced and most sustained intrusions into the lives of Christians occur in those countries— China, Vietnam and North Korea. (Cuba is the only other remaining communist nation.) In these countries, the methods of state control originally developed by Lenin in the Soviet Union remain operative.

North Korea is the most ruthless: Christianity is not allowed to exist except in 'show' communities developed for the few Western visitors. It is in Vietnam and China that Leninist principles, aided by very highly-developed cyber surveillance, are applied to keep Christians contained and controlled.

As mentioned above, China monitors all believers, but for very good historical reasons. A casual inspection of Chinese history shows that forces pressing for dynastic change have always first gathered in religious communities. With the vigorous contribution to the calls for democratisation coming from Christians in the north of China, especially in and around Beijing, an outside observer could easily conclude that China's leaders' historically founded fears are well placed.

In China and Vietnam the pattern is the same—the creation of networks of informants and spies inside communities, the checking of email and phone conversations, and the constant review of the performance of religious office holders by government officials. And from time to time, individuals are charged and convicted of 'crimes' that see them serving prison sentences, aimed as much at reforming the convicted 'criminal' as to strike fear into the hearts of Christians.

Belief is dangerous in both China and Vietnam.

Conclusion

The one thing about Christians in Asia you can be sure about is that no one tells the truth about how many Christians there are in most countries. The only exceptions are the Philippines and Timor-Leste because, in those countries, Christians are the majority population and have nothing to fear from telling the true story.

Part of the reason for the uncertainty over the numbers of Christians is the completely unreliable nature of national censuses in most Asian countries. But more significant is that those who could give accurate figures—the Christian Churches, who have baptismal registers—won't give accurate figures, because of the trouble they will create for themselves and their communities with governments and with extreme groups concerned about the growth of Christianity in Asian societies.

So, for the last three decades, the number of Catholics in China has been given as '12 million'; the number of Catholics in India has been given as somewhere between 17 and 30 million; and even in apparently serene and peaceful Thailand, the figure is always 300,000.

Ten years ago it was 300,000 and it will be the same in ten years' time, according to the retired Cardinal Archbishop of Bangkok.

Why is there this fear of disclosure? The answer is very simple: where Christians are a minority, the constant fear among them is that their growth in Asian societies will produce a violent backlash from fanatics in the majority non-Christian population.

The specter of persecution and the defensive behaviors that the fear of it produces are a given in Asian societies. That there are forces at work that make for the growth of Christianity in Asian societies – which many Christians would see as the work of the Holy Spirit – is undeniable. But just what is at work, and what those forces produce in Asian societies, is always ambiguous and uncertain. For example, Christianity has grown exponentially in the last four decades in South Korea, contradicting the common view that modernisation will do away with religious belief of all kinds. China is now predicted to have the largest Protestant population in the world by 2030.

And there are other countries in Asia where numerical trends in the growth of Christian populations have the potential to eclipse Christianity as a European phenomenon. In India, the growth of Christians among tribal and Dalit (formerly 'outcasts') communities is considerable.

But whatever unfolds, the current context of Asian societies and the politics that operate in them will mean that the persecution of growing minorities of Christians, who are alleged to destabilise social and political arrangements, will continue. And with that, so will persecution.

Bangladesh

Rock Ronald Rozario and Stephan Uttom
Dhaka

On October 5, 2015 three men pretending to be candidates for religious conversion knifed a Protestant pastor, Luke Sarkar, at his home in northern Pabna District. Sarkar, 50, of the Faith Bible Church, survived the murder attempt, but has lived in fear ever since.

A week after the attack, local police arrested five suspected members of a banned Islamic militant group, Jamaatul Mujahedin Bangladesh (JMB).

The motive for the attack on Sarkar is still unclear, but the link to Islamic fundamentalists is an unprecedented and fearsome twist in the story of religious persecution in Bangladesh.

On July 5, 2015, about 50 armed men attacked four Hindu villages at Baliadangi, Thakurgaon District, in order to evict the residents from their ancestral homes and agricultural land, which a local politician had been attempting to merge with his tea estate. Dozens of Hindu villagers fled their homes, and ten people were injured in the attack. More than three months after the attack, the victims had still not been able to return home, fearing further attacks from 'armed goons' of Dabirul Islam, a parliamentarian from the ruling Awami League. Most of the families took refuge in relatives' houses, and one family fled to India.

On July 24, 2014, police in Naogaon District exhumed the body of Ovidio Marandy, a Catholic from the indigenous Santal community, and a top land official, for a post-mortem, six months after his 'mysterious death'. Marandy, 32, was a vocal opponent of land grabs by local politicians from indigenous people. He disappeared from his workplace in Gaibandha District, and his family reject the 'road accident' story circulated by his opponents as the cause of his death. His post-mortem report has not yet seen daylight.

Such incidents of violence against religious and ethnic minorities are not uncommon in Muslim-majority Bangladesh, even though the country has a long tradition of religious and ethnic plurality and harmony.

A land of diversity and harmony

Present-day Bangladesh is the eastern part of greater Bengal, which included the Indian state of West Bengal, until the British partitioned India and Pakistan in 1947. Throughout history, Bengal was known as a land of many religions, cultures and ethnicities. After Partition, Muslim-majority East Bengal became the eastern wing of Pakistan, while Hindi-majority West Bengal joined India.

'At different times, different religions came to prominence. That might have created tensions at different times. But all those tensions were very short-lived. Throughout history, it is rather the case that unity, solidarity and understanding between communities, between ethnicities and religions, have been the major tradition,' said Professor Mesbah Kamal of the History Department, Dhaka University.

Sunni Muslims, mostly practicing a moderate form of Islam, make up 85 to 90 percent of Bangladesh's 160 million people. There are also small groups of other Islamic denominations like Shias, Ismaelis and Ahmadis. Hindus are the largest religious minority group, accounting for 8 percent of the population. The remainder profess adherence to Theravada Buddhism (0.05 percent) and Christianity (0.03 percent), mostly Catholicism. There are also indigenous religions and animism.

Bangladesh is an ethnically homogenous country, with over 99 percent of the people belonging to the Bengali race, the largest ethno-linguistic group in South Asia. However, there are also 3 million indigenous people from about 45 ethnic groups, mostly concentrated in the southeastern Chittagong Hill Tracts (CHT) and the north and northeast regions of the country. Indigenous people are mainly Buddhist or Christian, while some are Hindus and animists.

The legacy of colonialism and Islamisation

British rule in India is often blamed for sparking communal tensions, suspicions and violence between Hindus and Muslims – a by-product of a British-designed 'divide and rule' policy. Eventually, this led to the 1947 Partition of India on the basis of religion. Many critics now see this as a 'historic blunder.'

'The foundation of Pakistan in 1947 has been the most heinous political event in this country,' said Professor Kamal, who is chairman of the Dhaka-based Research and Development Collective, which specialises in studying ethnic and religious minority issues.

'From the foundation of Pakistan on August 14, 1947, the state used all of its power to not only disempower non-Muslims – Hindus, Christians and Buddhists – but also tried to expel them from the country. And this very communal intervention by the state has been responsible for the creation of an environment that is communally charged.'

During Pakistan's rule of Bangladesh from 1947 to 1971, religious minorities, especially Hindus, were persecuted by the state machinery and fundamentalist Islamic political forces. Hindus were seen as 'Indian agents' due to ongoing conflicts with India and an overarching anti-Indian sentiment.

Pakistan's government adopted its first constitution in 1956, and declared the country an Islamic state. It snatched away special land rights for indigenous people, in particular areas including the CHT and the northeast, which had been in place since the British period.

In 1965, Pakistan's military dictator, Ayub Khan, enacted a discriminatory property law, the Enemy Property Act, which saw the properties of an estimated 1.2 million Hindu families, worth US$55 billion, confiscated by the state in the following decades, according to a 2007 national study. This law was renamed the Vested Property Act in independent Bangladesh, and continued until its 2010 repeal by the Awami League government.

The Pakistan government's attempt at Islamisation of the state has been supported by Islamist and fundamentalist political parties including the Muslim League and Jamaat, both of which opposed Bangladeshi independence in 1971, and assisted the Pakistani army in the genocide of 3 million Bengali people during the independence war.

After their defeat in the war, the Islamists were temporarily shattered, but they revived after the assassination of Bangladesh's founding leader, Sheikh Mujibur Rahman, on August 15, 1975. The Islamists regrouped and thrived under the military government of Ziaur Rahman, who came to power in 1977 and later founded the center-right Bangladesh Nationalist Party (BNP). From the beginning, they have been funded by conservative Islamic countries in the Middle East including Saudi Arabia.

Rahman erased secularism, one of four key principles of the constitution, in an attempt to give an Islamic identity to the country, and replaced it with 'absolute trust and faith in Almighty Allah.' He also added the Islamic phrase '*Bismillahir-Rahmaanir Rahim*' ('In the name of Allah, the beneficent, the merciful') in the preamble of the constitution.

The process of Islamisation was continued by Rahman's successor, military dictator H.M. Ershad, who declared Islam the state religion in 1988.

The Awami League government reinstated secularism in the constitution in 2011, but did not change the state religion, fearing a political and Islamist backlash.

'Pakistan's government wanted to make the country an Islamic state, and wanted to cleanse minorities systematically, both politically and socially,' said Rana Dasgupta, a Hindu Supreme Court lawyer and secretary of the Bangladesh Hindu-Buddhist-Christian Unity Council.

'In Bangladesh, minorities are attacked for their land and political affiliation, but the governments all through these years have been negligent toward them,' he added.

Denial of ethnic plurality and discrimination

Due to the aggressive nationalism in the Bengali political leadership after Bangladesh's independence in 1971, ethnic plurality was denied in the 1972 constitution, although religious diversity was acknowledged.

The state only recognised the multi-ethnic composition of the country in a 2011 constitutional amendment, but termed indigenous people as 'minor races and tribal' and did not put them on an equal footing with Bengalis. As a result, influential Muslims, often politically-linked, attack and kill indigenous people, rape women, and vandalise their properties, in order to grab their land.

'The indigenous peoples are denied rights, their women are violated, and rape has become a systematic weapon to disempower and subjugate these people, and take their land. This denial of plurality, the denial of diversity, has created the foundation for atrocities against non-Bengali ethnic groups in the country,' said Professor Kamal.

In recent years, the government has even declared that there are 'no indigenous people in the country' and has forbidden political leaders and officials from attending programs held by or for indigenous people. It also refused to ratify the International Labour Organisation's (ILO) Convention 169, which includes the UN Declaration on the Rights of Indigenous Peoples.

'Bangladesh is obliged to sign and pass international laws, as it is a member of the United Nations. There are people in politics and government who are positive about indigenous people, but there is also a small but very strong anti-indigenous group that opposes the development agenda for indigenous people,' said Sanjeeb Drong, secretary of the Bangladesh Indigenous Peoples Forum.

Indigenous people in Bangladesh should be protected under a special law, with a separate land commission and monitoring department, he pointed out.

The curse of persecution

In Bangladesh, religious and ethnic minorities are persecuted for two reasons – political and social. Most of the minorities are considered a 'vote bank' for the nominally secular Awami League, the country's largest and current ruling political party.

The Awami League's rival BNP, and its long-time ally Jamaat, often target minorities for their support of the Awami League, both before and after general elections, in an attempt to reduce the minority vote.

In the 1990s, Hindus came under a series of attacks from Islamist fundamentalists over Hindu fundamentalists' demolition of the Babri Mosque in India. The attacks were backed by the then government of military dictator HM Ershad.

Before and after the 2001 election, which saw a BNP-Jamaat alliance sworn into power, Hindus came under more attacks, with dozens killed, Hindu women raped, and their houses and properties vandalised and looted.

In 2014, a judicial commission report found a total of 355 politically motivated murders, and 3,270 incidents of rape, arson, looting and other atrocities, largely against minorities, by BNP-Jamaat supporters.

Since 2012, Hindus have come under attack following death sentences and life prison sentences handed down to Islamist leaders, largely from Jamaat and also the BNP, by the war crimes tribunal, for their role during the 1971 war of independence. The violence so far has left about 10 Hindus dead.

Again, during a one-sided, controversial national election on January 5, 2014, which saw the Awami League win by default, Hindus were attacked by supporters of the BNP-Jamaat alliance for lining up to vote in an election they had boycotted.

Although targeted less, Christians have faced sporadic violence from Muslims—particularly during the Gulf War in the 1990s, and the US-led invasions of Iraq and Afghanistan.

In 1998, a Muslim mob, instigated and incited by Islamists, ransacked and vandalised several churches and Christian schools in the Luxmibazar area of Dhaka, over a land dispute. A Catholic school that owned the land was later forced to donate the disputed land to a local mosque.

In 2001, a Catholic church in Baniarchar was bombed by Islamic militants, killing 10 Catholics and injuring dozens. Police have so far failed to charge anyone.

'Christians are attacked for their land and property, and the attackers are backed by all political parties. They think Christians are a minuscule minority, weak and unable to protest and resist,' said Nirmol Rozario, secretary of the Bangladesh Christian Association.

'Religious conversion is legal in Bangladesh, but if a Muslim coverts to Christianity, the community will have serious problems from local Muslims. But if a Christian converts to Islam, it will get huge publicity,' he added.

Buddhists were almost untouched until three years ago. On September 29, 2012, a Muslim mob ransacked and burned down 19

Buddhist temples and 100 houses in the Ramu and Ukhiya areas of Cox's Bazar. They were reportedly angered by a Facebook image of a burnt Koran posted by a local Buddhist youth. The government rebuilt the temples and houses within a year after the worst anti-Buddhist riot in the country's history. About 18 cases were filed against the attackers, mostly local Islamists and political activists, but except for one case, police have failed to press charges.

Change in the ethnic and religious demography

The CHT, located near the Indian and Myanmar border, is home to over 25 ethnic indigenous groups, who are mostly Buddhist. Over the years, government-sponsored population transfer has changed the ethnic demography of the region and sparked sectarian violence between Bengali Muslim settlers and indigenous groups.

Indigenous people formed a militia group called Shanti Bahini, to resist settlers, and it waged a bush war against them and government forces for 25 years until a 1997 CHT Peace Accord. Years of violence saw hundreds of indigenous people killed and dozens of women raped at the hands of settlers and government forces.

Due to population transfer and violence, indigenous people have now become a minority in the CHT.

'In 1947, only 2 percent of people in the CHT were Bengali. Today, indigenous people account for less than 50 percent,' said Sanjeeb Drong. 'Many indigenous people have lost their land in violence, and also because of fake land documents provided by officials to Muslim settlers. This has forced many indigenous people to migrate to India and other countries,' he added.

In the north and northeastern plains, 140 indigenous people have been killed, over two dozen women raped, and about 10,000 people have migrated to India over the past forty years, according to the National Adivasi Forum. In 1971, religious minorities made up 23 percent of the country's population, but that figure stands at 9 percent today.

'Amid abuses related to property, Hindus have migrated to India over the years. No one wants to leave their homeland, but they have to leave because they see no future in this country,' said advocate Rana Dasgupta.

The culture of impunity

Bangladesh has no special law for the protection of religious and ethnic minorities. They do not have any reserved seats in parliament. Cases of violence against minorities are prosecuted in criminal courts, in the absence of special fast-track tribunals.

'For a long time we have demanded a special law to protect minorities, but no government has paid heed to our call. We have also asked for cases of violence against minorities to be handled in special courts, but this has also fallen on deaf ears,' said Dasgupta.

'In the absence of these special provisions, minorities don't get justice for violence [committed against them]. This culture of impunity encourages attackers,' he added.

Despite the government's restoration of Buddhist sites in Ramu and Ukhiya, Buddhist leaders are skeptical about justice. 'The culture of impunity against attackers of minorities has been in place for a long time. We don't see justice after communal attacks. Sometimes there are police investigations and judicial probes into the violence, but justice is delayed, and often denied,' said barrister Biplab Barua, a member of the Bangladesh Buddhist Federation.

The revival of religious extremism

Since 2001, Bangladesh has seen a sharp rise in Islamic militancy across the country, with extremist groups carrying out bomb attacks, and torturing and killing people publically, to press for the introduction of sharia law.

Amid a massive national and international outcry, the government has cracked down on militants, and arrested and executed their top leaders. It has also banned two major militant groups, Harkat-ul-Jihad and Jamaatul Mujahedin Bangladesh.

However, religious extremism has not been eradicated. Since 2013, five secular bloggers have been murdered and several others injured in brutal attacks by militants, who aim to deliver a chilling message to secular and atheist bloggers, many of whom have been forced to flee to Europe and America. Many link the attackers with Islamist parties like Jamaat, whose entire leadership is facing charges at the war crimes tribunal for atrocities in the 1971 war.

In 2013, fundamentalist group Hefazat-e-Islam, allegedly linked to Jamaat, marched in Dhaka, with over a million Muslims taking part, to press the Awami League government on 13 staunchly Islamic demands, including a blasphemy law and the execution of atheist bloggers.

This was in response to a massive Shahbagh protest movement organized by young secularists demanding the death penalty for those convicted of war crimes in 1971, and a ban on religion-based politics.

'Bangladesh is a democracy and everyone has the right to freedom of expression, including atheists, and the government needs to protect them,' said Professor Kamal. 'Not all of the bloggers are atheists, but they are being branded as atheists because they support the war crimes trial and hate the politicisation of religion.'

The way forward

Professor Kamal pointed out several steps that the government can take to ensure the rights and dignity of people of all religions and ethnicities. 'The [notion of a] state religion, [in this case] Islam, must go, and the government should give equal status to all religions in the constitution. The indigenous peoples must be recognised by the constitution, along with their land rights, and their traditional community rights must be established. And religious freedom and bloggers should be defended, even if they are atheists,' he said.

Minorities need political representation to ensure rights and justice, said advocate Dasgupta. 'There must be 60 reserved [parliamentary] seats for minorities, and a minority affairs ministry. There should be a special law to protect minority rights, and a special tribunal to deliver justice in cases of violence against minorities,' he pointed out.

China
Religious Freedom in China

ucanews.com reporter, Beijing

On a residential street in Turpan, a sweltering oasis town in western China's Xinjiang region, restrictions on religion are all too graphic. A red banner hung by authorities on a traditional Muslim Uighur home urges residents to inform police about illegal acts—a reference to banned religious and separatist activity.

Further down the street, a mosque is monitored by a CCTV camera that rotates 360 degrees. Two young children play in the mosque doorway under the gaze of the camera, which moves—apparently under remote control—to scan the neighborhood. On the mosque's front gate, a sign warns that minors are not allowed to enter.

'I want my children to pray with me,' said one Muslim Uighur after Friday prayers at another mosque in Turpan. 'How are our children supposed to learn from the Koran if they are not allowed inside mosques?'

Restive areas like Xinjiang and Tibet remain at the sharp end of China's constraining religious policies, a side-effect of Communist Party efforts to stamp out dissent. In a bid to pacify, Beijing has created a web of laws, directives and other bureaucratic instruments that have in recent years narrowed the space for many groups to worship.

Recent violence in western China, led by Uighur separatists, means this minority of roughly 12 million people has become a key target for Chinese authorities. Xinjiang is the only region in China where minors are not allowed to attend mosques. Although this has been policy since 1980, the rule was more strictly enforced after 9/11 and again amid the war against Islamic State, said Alim Seytoff, executive director of the Uighur Human Rights Project in Washington, D.C. This new political climate gave Beijing the perfect excuse to tackle resistance to its rule among Uighurs, he said.

"The motivation of the Chinese authorities in banning Islamic worship by Uighur minors is to dilute their Uighur identity, secularise and eventually assimilate them into China's communist, atheist, materialist society," added Seytoff.

Efforts to control Uighur children's access to Islamic teaching has intensified amid a recent upsurge in separatist violence that left hundreds of people dead last year.

Authorities detained 85 people and 'rescued' 190 children from underground madrassas in raids across Xinjiang reported the state-run *Legal Daily* in September 2015. It remains unclear whether anyone was convicted. Public notices in Xinjiang warn that leading minors in religious activities incurs prison terms of between three and seven years.

In Xian, a major city further east, outside of Xinjiang in Shaanxi Province, the roughly 50,000 minority Muslim Hui are free to bring their children to mosques. The same ethnic group is not able to do so in Xinjiang, where tighter rules appear aimed at containing the separatist threat Beijing sees in the Uighurs.

In the past, China's efforts to link this ethnic minority to international Islamic terrorism were ignored as fantasy outside of China. However, Chinese nationals have reportedly turned up fighting for the group calling itself Islamic State (IS) in Iraq and Syria in recent years, and in August 2015 a bombing in central Bangkok that killed 20 people led to the arrest of two Uighurs. The two suspects were due to face trial in Thailand.

'There are links to international terrorism but still not to the extent claimed by the Chinese government,' said Nicholas Bequelin, Amnesty International's East Asia director, based in Hong Kong.

As a result, Uighurs complain they face a tougher task joining the annual pilgrimage to Mecca. All Chinese who go on the Hajj are required by law to join a state-approved tour. Uighurs say they often find it hard even getting a passport. This in turn has prompted a trade in fake ID documents. In Urumqi, the regional capital of Xinjiang, this reporter was handed a flyer in the main Uighur quarter advertising fake marriage certificates, ID cards and driving licenses.

At the ground level, Beijing's claim of terrorist links between Uighurs and overseas Islamic groups has driven ever stricter efforts to control access to the Koran—Islam's holy book.

In 2014, the state-run Xinjiang Islamic Institute, the only body allowed to train Islamic religious leaders, began a US$48 million expansion, with plans for teaching 1,000 students per year by 2017. Although this represents increased capacity to send imams out across Xinjiang – on the surface enabling religious education – the primary motivation has been tackling religious extremism.

'The extremists often start by teaching people about the parts of the Koran that have never been mentioned by their imams, and then inject violent thoughts in people by misrepresenting doctrines,' Abudulkrep Tumniaz, deputy director of the Xinjiang Islamic Institute, told the state-run *China Daily* in March. 'Our institute aims to prepare respectful, knowledgeable religious leaders who can lead the Muslims of Xinjiang in the right direction.'

This cocktail of measures designed to curb violence and separatism has led to a narrowing of the definition of legal religious activity. Public notices in Xinjiang warn that having dinner with someone talking about the Koran who is not a registered Islamic instructor is forbidden. Other signs state that young men are not allowed to wear 'large beards' or women face-covering burqas. Rewards of up to 5,000 yuan (US$800) are offered for those who inform.

In January 2015, Urumqi officially banned burqas. Then, in March, a court in Kashgar, a city in the Xinjiang Uighur Autonomous Region, with a majority Uighur population, sentenced a 38-year-old man to six years in prison for growing a beard. His wife was given two years for wearing an Islamic veil. The court announced that both were found guilty of 'picking quarrels and provoking trouble,' a catch-all charge in China for anything deemed a challenge to state authority.

Party officials have sought out veiled women for 're-education' in the countryside. Rewards for women who remove their burqas include expenses-paid holidays to Beijing and Shanghai, noted Timothy Grose, assistant professor of China studies at the Rose-Hulman Institute of Technology in Indiana.

'The CCP [Communist Party of China] is attempting to promote alternative forms of Uighur dress—namely *atlas* [a type of patterned silk], *doppa* [embroidered cap] and braided hair—which it claims are appropriate expressions of Uighur ethnic beauty,' said Grose, who is researching trends in Islamic dress in Xinjiang. 'Yet the logic here is paradoxical, since the styles the CCP deems to be 'modern' and 'normal' are considered by many young Uighur women to be 'traditional' or even 'old fashioned,' and out of touch with current fashion. In other words, some women decide to wear the veil in order to leap forward into a transnational Islamic community, and not step back in time.'

Yet more new laws look set to further narrow the space for Uighur religious and cultural practices. In July 2015, Chinese legislators began drafting an amendment banning 'terrorist clothing,' according to the state-run *Global Times*.

'In terms of the distinction between normal religious activities and abnormal religious activities, this cursor is placed differently in different situations, different provinces and different localities and different religions,' said Bequelin.

Since Chairman Mao, when religion was essentially banned, China has generally seen an opening of religious space, he added. But recent tensions with Uighurs means the trend is going the other way in Xinjiang, said Bequelin. So too in Tibet, where resistance to Han-Chinese rule also persists. Rebellions in recent decades have mostly started in Tibetan Buddhist monasteries, which remain a key target of authorities. Chinese police have recently arrested a number of teenage monks.

Lobsang Jamyang, 15, a monk from Kirti monastery in Ngabawas detained in September 2015 after he walked through the town shouting, 'Invite his holiness the Dalai Lama to Tibet.'Another 19-year-old monk was arrested from the same monastery a few weeks earlier, following a similar protest, reported London-based advocacy group Free Tibet.

These cases both occurred among Tibetan communities in Sichuan Province. Inside Tibet proper, restrictions against monks and nuns are reportedly stricter, but information is more difficult to come by amid tight security. In 2014, more than 100 nuns were reportedly expelled from a convent in Dhingri County in Shigatse Prefecture.

Gyaltsen Norbu, the Panchen Lama hand picked by Beijing, made a rare, thinly veiled critique of China's policy on Tibetan monasteries and nunneries during a speech in Beijing in March 2015. Noting the dwindling numbers of monks and nuns—a reference to China's rarely acknowledged quotas on monks and nuns—the 11th Panchen Lama warned there is a danger of Buddhism 'existing in name only.'

Norbu was selected by Beijing in 1995 to replace GendunChoekyiNyima, the choice of the Dalai Lama as the next Panchen Lama. The government has said it also intends to control the reincarnation of the Dalai Lama himself, a move Beijing sees as the endgame in crushing Tibetan resistance.

Turning 80 years old in July 2015, the Dalai Lama has said he may not anoint a successor, thereby ending the lama lineage, a move that has angered government amid a war of words over the issue.

'Every step has to be reported to the central government and get approval,' Zhu Weiqun, chairman of the Ethnic and Religious Committee, said in March 2015.

In recent years, Beijing has ended all communication with Tibet's exiled government, which in turn has spurred a new cycle of religious restrictions as Beijing seeks to choke discourse that counters its steadfast position.

Authorities finished installing televisions in every one of Tibet's nearly 1,800 Buddhist monasteries in June 2015, according to the state-run *Tibet Daily*. As part of the same program, authorities removed 'illegal' satellite television systems that beamed in news from outside of Tibet, many with updates on the Dalai Lama. Authorities have also insisted that each monastery flies China's national flag, and monks and nuns now receive lessons from the Party on Chinese law.

'They are trying to control the monastic institution,' saidTsering Tsomo, executive director of the Tibetan Center for Human Rights and Democracy based in Dharamsala, northern India. 'It's all about controlling and all about modifying this sect of Buddhism.'

Efforts to deny outside sources of information have combined with a renewed security effort on the Tibetan border, whereby Beijing has funded guards on the Nepal side of the frontier, said Tsomo. Before a Tibetan uprising in 2008, a few thousand Tibetans managed to escape each year through the Himalayas. Increased border security since, means numbers have dropped to just a few hundred.

GologJigme, a former monk, is among the few who have made it out of China following a daring escape in May 2014. After making a film soliciting views on the Dalai Lama from dozens of ordinary

Tibetans, he was arrested and tortured numerous times since 2008 before he eventually went on the run for over a year and slipped across the border to Dharamsala.

Now living in Switzerland, Gologrecounted how hundreds of Chinese police raided his former monastery in a Tibetan area of Qinghai Province in 2008.

'All portraits of the Dalai Lama were burned, or smashed with their feet or their weapons,' he said.

Chinese efforts to separate Tibetans from the Dalai Lama remain counter-productive, he said: trampling on cultural and religious traditions only prompts greater resistance.'They are showing that we can't live under them,' he adds.

In recent years, Chinese President Xi Jinping has talked up Buddhism. This is just a smokescreen as part of the efforts to eradicate ethnic minority and foreign religions, including Christianity, argues Golog.

China's president continues to quote regularly from traditional Chinese religions, particularly Confucianism. However, this has been misinterpreted, said Sebastian Billioud, a professor of anthropology of religion at Paris Diderot University.

In a book published in September 2015, *The Sage and the People: The Confucian Revival in China*, Billioud said surveys show grassroots Confucianism resurfaced in China long before Xi became leader of the Communist Party in late 2012.

'I think that what the central authorities are promoting is a kind of new ideological cocktail in which traditional culture is definitely important but also diverse and combined with lot of other elements as well – including remnants of revamped 'Red' ideology,' he said.

Where exactly Xi's position stands on religion remains heavily debated. China's president was due to chair a meeting on religion in October 2015, but this appears to have been postponed again, said Fenggang Yang, director of the Center on Religion and Chinese Society at Purdue University.

'Xi might not be happy with the current policy, but he seems not happy with suggestions from the existing advisors either,' said Fenggang. 'He needs to reach out beyond the existing theoreticians to come up with a sensible policy towards religion.'

Christianity in China

Religious persecution can be said to be 'no news' to Christians in China. This has been true since the Communist Party took over the country in 1949.

Before the turn of the millennium, persecution of Christians came in the form of torture or detention without trial. Up to the 1990s, some Catholic priests of the underground Church—that not recognised by the government—recall being beaten, undergoing forced injections of medication for alleged mental illness, and suffering cold water being poured over them in freezing winter.

Since 2000, instances of this kind of torture have been less frequent, but detention without trial is still a common occurrence.

A change of tactics

'The authorities realised that violent crackdowns only produce martyrs or heroes for the Church. This is contrary to what the regime wants,' explained Or Yan-yan, project officer at the Hong Kong Catholic Diocese's Justice and Peace Commission.

'The regime also began to care about its world image, and wanted to show its soft power in order to enter the world arena,' Or said, 'adding that its aim to control never changes.'

Patrick Poon Kar-wai, a China researcher for Amnesty International, believes it is not easy to make comparisons between past and present, as Chinese society is so different now due to economic growth and advancements in telecommunications.

'It is a different form of persecution. The regime accused dissidents of counter-revolutionary crimes in the past. Now, it is 'pocket crime', he said.

'That is, they would charge you with 'provocation' crimes, or they would hold people in secret detention so that they didn't need to inform a lawyer or the person's family,' Poon said.

Zhong Dao, a Protestant writer in China, has observed the differences in persecution, over time, from the political viewpoint. 'The current political struggles between various camps in the Party is an obvious characteristic of persecution today. This has not been seen in the past.'

Disguised persecution

Persecution comes in a disguised form nowadays.

'They are skillful at using terms related to universal values. However, one has to be careful as the Communist Party distorts the essence of these values,' Or Yan-yan said.

For instance, the Chinese Catholic Patriotic Association (CCPA) is also-called Church entity, but the authorities use it to control the Church, even though this is described as 'democratic management of the Church.'

'So people [are led to] think it is good and progressive. Those who oppose it are 'wrong' or labelled as conservative,' Or said.

As an example, a cross-demolition campaign was initiated in Zhejiang Province in late 2013. The official line was that it was removing illegal religious structures, with the excuse of a 'Three Rectifications and One Demolition' project for city planning. Although all denominations suffered from demolition of their properties, the city planning project was never convincing, as it focused more on the Protestant Church.

This eastern coastal province has an estimated Christian population of 2 million, including about 210,000 Catholics. By 2015, about 1,500 crosses had been removed, with the majority belonging to Protestant churches.

This fact may help explain the feelings of Zhong Leqin, a Protestant preacher who now resides in the United States, upon witnessing the cross-removal program in his Wenzhou hometown.

'Persecution is particularly ridiculous in the 21st century … it is like living medieval times,' said Zheng, who has been keeping track of the number of church crosses demolished, and reporting this news on social media for Chinese Christians since early 2014.

However, even into 2015, the authorities seemed not to care about laying bare this brutality in front of the public.

'We have seen more severe persecution than in the past few years. The cross-removal campaign has continued for about two years, but[in 2015] there was also the arrest of a dozen Protestant pastors and their lawyers who took their cases to court,' Patrick Poon said.

Creating division

The scale of the crackdown in Zhejiang was so unprecedented that some observers believed it was related to the growth of Christianity in the area, and the projection by Yang Fenggang, a Chinese scholar at Purdue University in the United States, that China would be the largest Christian country in the world by 2030.

The projection of 248 million Christians was almost a ten-fold increase from the statistical record of the Chinese Academy of Social Sciences in 2010. The Beijing think-tank gave the Protestant population at 23 million, accounting for 1.8 percent of the total 1.3 billion population, following a survey across China. The Holy Spirit Study Centre, a research center of the Hong Kong Diocese, estimated the Catholic population at 8–10 million in 2014.

'Extreme left ideology is on the rise. The rulers fear that if Christianity continues to develop, it will threaten their dialectical materialism,' said a priest in Hebei Province who only identified himself as Father Peter.

Father Peter, who formerly belonged to the underground Church, understands well the tactic of dividing the Church community in order to weaken its bonds.

Hebei is a strong hold of the Catholic Church in China, where there is an estimated 1 million Catholic population. As in other provinces across China, the Catholic population is divided into the government-sanctioned official Church, and the underground Church. It is the same story in the Protestant Church, with the house Church an equivalent to the underground Catholic Church.

'The Chinese communists have worried about peaceful evolution ever since the Soviet Union dissolved and the dramatic changes in Eastern Europe,' said Father Peter. 'It is impossible for the regime to let go of its control on religions. It will curb religious development from the root,' he said.

To some extent, the Vatican's China policy is also a source of division, despite some in the Church denying that.

While the Holy See insists that the government-sanctioned CCPA —its constitution stipulates the principle of an independent Church —is incompatible with Catholic doctrine, it continues to appoint bishops who hold positions in the association.

Some laypeople see their bishops as not loyal and brave enough to follow the Church's teaching, while the bishops think they cannot do much under China's political reality.

As China has not shown much improvement in religious freedom, a certain portion of Catholics in both the open and underground Churches do not support China-Vatican talks, as they see the timing as not right. They do not believe China will change, even if it signs agreements to build ties.

Changing Christianity's doctrines

In late 2014, following repeated clashes between security forces and Christians who were defending their church crosses in Zhejiang, the authorities introduced the 'Wu Hua, Wu Jin' ('Five Introductions and Five Approaches')policy on religious policy and regulations, the healthcare system, general scientific culture, poverty alleviation, and harmonious development for Church congregations.

This move did not garner much attention outside China, but a July 24, 2015 report in *Zhongguo Minzhu Bao*, a newspaper run by the State Commission for Ethnic Affairs, justified the policy by saying that many Christians did not know the relevant law, or understand the government policy of removing illegal religious structures.

The 'Wu Hua, Wu Jin' approach is to localise religions, standardise management, indigenise theology, publicise finance, and adapt doctrines to local contexts.

The effect? One church in Zhejiang was told to provide a home service for the aged under the 'Wu Hua, Wu Jin' policy.

'The public might think this is a charitable service that the church community should accept. In fact, it ignores the fact that it is a venue for religious gatherings,' Or said.

'Christians may not accept this, based on their understanding of what a church means,' she said, noting that it will eventually give way to conflict and confrontation between the Christians and non-Christians.

Another more serious effect is on adapting doctrine to local contexts, and indigenising theology. The discussion has been ongoing for years in Protestant circles. The latest seminar on 'Chinalisation of the Protestant Church' was held in September 2015.

Catholics are also alert to 'Chinalisation' being introduced to the Catholic Church in China. In a series of analytical articles, a Catholic scholar with the pen-name Wu Moyan points out that 'Chinalisation' is different from Church jargon 'localisation' or 'inculturation' as it bears a political resonance.

Father Peter said that, under the 'Chinalisation' call by President Xi Jinping, changing doctrine might affect churches, as they are often regarded as 'foreign' influences that are subject to the control of foreign states like the Vatican.

Pessimistic but with hope

It seems that very few observers see a positive outlook for Christians under Xi Jinping's administration, which could last for seven more years if everything goes fine. 'Xi is like Mao Zedong. He likes power and dictatorship compared to other Politburo members in the standing committee,' said Patrick Poon.

'In the two years after Xi assumed power, the arrest of dissenters became more serious than under Hu Jintao. I do not see improvement as being likely in the near future,' said Poon.

Or Yan-yan also sees control being tightened, and not just on religions. 'I am particularly worried that the 'Wu Jin, Wu Hua' policy will be introduced to other provinces.'

Zhong Dao notes three points for the future: the political direction of the Party-State, the strength and maturity of the Church, and the ethnic characteristics in individual regions. The Protestant writer said that in the reality of the Internet era, controlling through a culture of fear is no longer of no use. 'People have transcended from 60 years of persecution. It is hard to have entire unity. However, religion has never taken on a mainstream role in China. It will not in the future, unless there is a fundamental change in national characteristics, which I think is only possible with God's will,' he said.

Although preacher Zheng Leguo agrees that controls may tighten in the next few years, he remains hopeful. 'The authorities will eventually find that they cannot get any result from controlling the development of Christian Churches,' he said. 'But it remains for the faithful communities to fight for their own religious freedom.'

China's development could not be completely removed from international society, and the leadership also cares about its international image. 'As long as the Vatican upholds its principles, it will win the respect of China. Then, diplomatic ties will become something that the Chinese authorities expect and strive for, and in return that will benefit Christianity in China as a whole,' said Zheng.

India

By ucanews.com reporter in New Delhi

On March 14, 2015, a 74-year-old nun was raped inside a convent near the eastern Indian city of Kolkata. Police arrested six people, most of them Muslims, who they say attacked the nun after they robbed the convent.

On June 20, 2015, a 48-year-old Catholic nun was raped as she slept insider her convent-run medical dispensary in Raipur, Chhattisgarh State, in northeastern India. Police arrested two people four months later and said the crime was committed under influence of alcohol.

On September 28, 2015, a 52-year-old Muslim man, Akhlaq Ahmed, was beaten to death in the village of Bisahra in Uttar Pradesh State, 60 kilometers south of New Delhi, after rumors spread that he and his family ate beef.

These crimes, ay leaders of Christian communities, are planned attacks that are part of a wider conspiracy against religious minorities since the pro-Hindu BJP, or Bharatiya Janata Party (Indian People's Party), came to power in New Delhi in May 2014.

The BJP is widely seen as a party that supports the Hindutva ideology of Hindu groups that work to make India a Hindu theocratic nation.

'The Hindu groups are much more emboldened [after the BJP victory] and are openly supporting the Hindutva ideology,' said Richard Howell, general secretary of the Evangelical Fellowship of India.

'Christians and even Muslims are targeted not because of our work or religion, but because our religious identity does not fit into the ideology of one nation, one culture, and one people,' according to Christian leaders like Howell.

Asaduddin Owaisi, a Muslim political leader, has gone on record to say that incidents like the lynching of a Muslim man in Uttar Pradesh in September 2015—allegedly for eating beef—are part of a planned attack on Muslims. 'Those who say this [the lynching]is an accident are trying to protect those who planned and executed it.'

In the recent past there have been hate speeches from some Hindu leaders demanding that Muslims and Christians leave India and go to nations where they are in the majority. These attempts by fanatical groups to project India as a nation only of Hindus go on despite the country having a secular, socialist, democratic constitution, which asserts that all Indians 'are equally entitled to freedom of conscience and the right to freely profess, practice and propagate' any religion of their choice.

The religious minorities are not asking for any favors, but want to ensure that human rights enshrined in the constitution are upheld. 'Give us the protection that is the right of every citizen of the country,' Howell said.

However, Surendra Jain, joint general secretary of Vishwa Hindu Parishad (the World Hindu Council), said the Christian complaints about persecution in India are baseless and a tactic to attract international support and funding for their activities.

There is also a political plot behind the claims by Christians of persecution, according to Jain. 'The reason is very clear, that they [Christians]want to politicise the issue of persecution. They start complaining about persecution whenever a [BJP] government comes to power, and blame the Hindu groups for atrocities,' he said.

Political discussions and policy decisions in India are now, more than ever, seen through the prism of religion. Muslims and Christians look at government actions and omissions, and are suspicious of the Hindutva ideology.

Howell said Hindu groups working for a theocratic nation consider Christians, Muslims and Parsis as non-Indic religions. 'Our culture is not treated as an Indian or Hindu culture, as understood by the Hindutva groups,' he said.

He and Samuel Jaikumar of the National Council of Churches in India share the view that the fanatical campaigners spread a fear that

Christians are 'enemies of Hindus' who will convert all Indians to Christianity unless opposed. Jaikumar said that the government has 'to walk the extra mile' to protect India's Muslims and Christians.

The violence against minorities is also engineered to project Hindu groups as the protectors of religion and nation, in order to consolidate a Hindu majority of votes, according to some Christian leaders.

However, it is wrong to project all Hindus in India as anti-Christian and anti-Muslim, said Cardinal Baselios Cleemis, president of the Indian Catholic bishops. 'The vast majority of Hindus in this country are secular, peace-loving and admirers of the religious and cultural diversity of this land. The country continues to be secular and democratic because of its peoples' respect for each other. Only a very small section of Hindus are fanatics, and create trouble,' Cardinal Cleemis said.

Increasing attacks

Christian and Muslim leaders reiterate that the BJP taking power in New Delhi has given a fresh impetus to hardliners, who see the political victory as a mandate to implement their ideology of building a Hindu nation.

Rights activists and secular groups in New Delhi released a document in March 2015 saying they have documented at least 43 deaths in over 600 cases of religious violence in India, 149 targeting Christians and the rest Muslims, in 2014 and up until March 2015.

Ever since the BJP came to power with Narendra Modi as prime minister, 'there has been a relentless foregrounding of communal identities, a ceaseless attempt to create a divide between us and them. The BJP leaders are guaranteed to abuse, ridicule and threaten minorities,' according to the document released by the rights activists.

The document said violence peaked between August and October 2014, with 56 cases, with a further 25 cases during the Christmas season, including the burning of a Catholic church in eastern New Delhi. The violence continued well into 2015.

According to the report, much of the violence, 54 percent of the reported cases, consists of threats, intimidation and coercion, often with the police looking on. Physical violence constituted a quarter of all cases (24 percent), and violence against Christian women—a trend that is increasingly being seen since anti-Christian riots in Kandhamal, Odisha in 2007 and 2008—was at 11 percent.

'Breaking of statues and the Cross, and other acts of desecration, were recorded in about 8 percent of the cases, but many more were also consequent to other forms of violence against institutions,' the document said.

Much of the violence was in northern states, where Christians are a tiny minority, and where BJP governments are in power. In these states, almost all Christians are tribal or Dalit ('oppressed') people, who have lived in servitude and subjugation for centuries.

Christian leaders say that Hindu hardliners fear tribal and lower-caste people becoming ducated, which could lead them not only to stop slaving for upper-caste Hindus, but also to question the idea of high-caste superiority. Political groups also have vested interests in keeping the poor uneducated, Church leaders allege.

No one had been arrested four months after the nun was raped in Raipur in the BJP-ruled Chhattisgarh State, said Father Sebastian Poomattathil, vicar general of Raipur Archdiocese. This despite the National Human Rights Commission stating publically that police had mishandled the investigation, he added.

'We all know what is happening. They want to scare away Christian missionaries from these areas in northern India, where Christians are a tiny minority and work among tribal and lower-caste Dalit people.'

The history of religious-based hate

The Islamophobiaamong Indian Hindus, and the BJP's rise to political prominence, are intrinsically linked to the history of India, particularly to Zahir-ud-Din Muhammad Babur, commonly known as Babur, who invaded India in 1526 and laid the foundations of the Moghul Muslim dynasty.

Muslims from Central Asia began invading and conquering India in the 12th century. The invading powers plundered villages, killed the men, raped women, destroyed temples to convert them to mosques, and subjugated the people. History has witnessed generations of Hindus and Muslims passing on centuries of mutual fear, disparagement and hatred, all of which finally resulted in the partition of the subcontinent in 1947 on the basis of religion. The partition and the resultant bloodbath left between 200,000 and 500,000 people dead, in one of history's worst episodes of religious-based violence.

The persecution of Christians is inexorably tied up with Hindu-Muslim relations in colonial India.

'Northern India, especially western Uttar Pradesh, Haryana, and Delhi, became home to Hindu refugees who had been victims of violence by Muslims. This memory has shaped north Indian politics since 1947,' said John Dayal, a member of the National Integration Council and a former president of the All-India Catholic Union.

The pain and bloodshed of Partition were still fresh in the minds of many Indians, as stories of how fathers, mothers and siblings were attacked and killed, were passed on to subsequent generations. A collective social psyche of hatred towards Muslims developed in northern India, which bore the brunt of Partition's ravages.

The constitution—which had begun to be formulated before Partition, but was completed after the mayhem—itself reflects the Hindu majority, evidenced in such things as the call for a common civil code, and an aversion to alcohol and the slaughter of cows, although it was orthodox Hindus who rebelled against serious reforms to Hindu personal law, said Dayal.

Some current senior Indian politicians were children when they witnessed the death, forced migration and homelessness that Partition meant for thousands of Hindus who fled the newly formed Pakistan. One of them is now retired leader of the BJP, Lal Kishen Advani, 88, who studied in Karachi's St. Patrick's School and lived in the Pakistani port city until Partition forced his family to flee to India.

Advani, a long-time member of the hardline Hindu Rashtriya Swayam Sevan Sangh (RSS), an umbrella body for several pro-Hindu organisations, was also a leader of Bharatiya Jan Sangh, the first incarnation of the present BJP. In 1990, Advani began a campaign to mobilise people to build a temple in Ayodhya, the birthplace of the Hindu lord Rama, in the process demolishing a disputed structure called the Babri Mosque. Advani and other BJP leaders claimed Babur, the first Moghul emperor, built the mosque after destroying a Ram temple on the site, and the mosque had long epitomised a Muslim insult toward Hindus. On December 6, 1992, a frenzied mob demolished the mosque, which resulted in nationwide riots that left some 2,000 people, mostly Muslims, dead. The incident also accelerated the BJP's rise to power.

The BJP could win only two seats in the 1984 general election, but seven years after the Ayodhya riots, in 1999, with the promise of building a temple in Ayodhya, the party won 183 seats in the 543-seat House, and took power after forming a coalition government. In the next two elections, in 2004 and 2009, the party did not win enough seats to take power, but in the 2014 election it won a landslide of 282 seats, which Hindu leaders interpreted as a mandate to implement Hindutva ideology.

'Once the Hindu masses are radicalised, we have a potentially dangerous situation affecting all religious minorities. The RSS has always held Muslims, Christians and communists as enemies of the Hindu *rashtra* ('nation'), and therefore enemies of modern India,' Dayal said.

These groups see evangelisation as cultural violence and a means to overwhelm Hindus, Dayal explained. 'It is all so much street logic and not based on facts, or reason, but it often succeeds in brainwashing and rousing young people who are unemployed or who see everyone else as a roadblock to their own economic and social progress. That is the ideological, economic, social and political backbone of what we call communalism.'

The mosaic of complexities

The religious-based violence in India should be seen against the backdrop of its burgeoning population and socio-political issues. India is one of the world's most densely populated countries, and the second most populous nation on earth after China. With a population of 1.2 billion people, it is expected to become the most populous nation by the middle of this century. It covers just 2.4 percent of world's land area, but is home to more than 17.5 percent of the global population.

Human life is cheap here, and violence and riots are not considered serious unless hundreds are dead. A few deaths cannot shock people in a country where thousands are killed daily. Government data showed that 1,200 people died in accidents in 2014. Daily, some 360 people commit suicide. According to United Nations estimates, every year 2.1 million Indian children die before reaching the age of five; four every minute. On each day, tuberculosis alone kills an average of 1,000 people. One murder, even if for reasons of faith or religion, may not make a headline.

Every two seconds, a baby is born in India, and the population explosion carries with it the usual problems of poverty, illiteracy and an associated lack of self-worth. At least 320 million people cannot afford one full meal a day; 260 million cannot read or write their names, most of them women; and nearly 700 million live in homes without lavatories. Every day, at least at least 100 women are raped, and three times that number are sexually assaulted, according to official government records. Thousands of crimes, especially in villages, go unreported. Even the rape of a nun cannot shock a great many Indians.

Police and officials see offenses against Christians and Muslims as just normal cases of crime in a country where, official records show, close to 100 people are murdered every day, and an equal number of attempted murders are reported. It is therefore easy for officials to see criminal trespass and robberies of churches and Muslim institutions as simply part of the more than 1,700 similar crimes happening across the nation on a daily basis.

That gives seeming credibility to Jain's argument that more temples are attacked in India than churches or mosques. 'Christians complain of attacks on churches in Delhi [in 2014]. But investigations have proved that only three churches were attacked, and those too for small thefts.'He said some 300 temples have been attacked in the country in the last two years.

The sociology of Christian hate

Opposition to Christianity and missions is primarily sociological, according to Catholic leaders such as Archbishop Leo Cornelio of Bhopal, who is based in the state capital of central Madhya Pradesh State.

The social philosophy of the country is mostly built on the classification of society into a four-tier caste system of Brahmins (priests), Kshatriyas (warriors),Vaishyas (traders) and Shudra (servants). The servant class and those outside the caste system were considered untouchable.

'But Christianity does not believe in such practices. It preaches quality and justice for all, and this infuriates those with different ideologies, like the high-caste Hindus. They oppose Christianity because they see it as threat to their social system,' Archbishop Cornelio explained.

'The Church's social welfare activities, especially education activities, are seen as challenging a traditionalist system in which it is easy to exploit the millions of poor tribal and Dalit people as servants,' he said.

Although the caste system is now outlawed, discrimination against those outside the four superior castes continues in several ways. The socially poor Dalit and tribal people, many of them Christians, are still victimised, and many of them lack basic housing and food. Young Dalit and tribal people are also trafficked to cities and sexually exploited. The missionaries interventions on their behalf are seen as a challenge to upper-caste dominance, Christian leaders allege.

Communal hate, violence and terrorism are violations of the law, Dayal said. But the tweaking of the law sometimes encourages and makes it easy to rouse people against religious minorities, and the Dalits and tribals in particular. For instance, a presidential order of 1950 took away the freedom of Dalits to choose their religion, essentially meaning that they would lose all constitutional affirmative action and privileges if they became Muslim or Christian.

Successive governments have refused to undo this order, and the BJP has categorically said that it will not allow constitutional benefits —such as quotas for jobs and education, meant to uplift the poorer classes—to go to Christians of Dalit origin because Christianity does not follow the caste system, and the term Dalit Christian is self-contradictory. Christian leaders such as Dayal say the BJP's stance is based on the fear that granting quotas will encourage more Dalits to convert to Christianity.

The challenge to diversity

Indian Christians are as diverse among themselves, in terms of languages and culture, as all of India's peoples are. Indians speak 415 living languages. The country officially recognises 22 languages, each of them having more than 1 million native speakers. Hindi and English are the official languages, but communication can be a huge issue, as most villagers do not understand standardised Hindi or English. Language has become, by default, the main ethnic identifier for most Indians.

This ancient land of rajas and maharajas became a country as it stands today only in 1947, when it became politically independent of British rule. Following independence in 1947, India's ethnically, linguistically and culturally different states came together to form a federation of 28 states. The diversity of religions further complicates the social life of a country that is the birthplace of Hinduism, Buddhism, Sikhism and Jainism. According to the 2001 census, 80.5 percent of India's 1.02 billion people are Hindus. With some 138 million Muslims (13.5 percent), India is also the third-largest Muslim country in the world after Indonesia and Pakistan.

Christianity, withapproximately28 million followers (2.4 percent), is the second-largest minority religion, followed by Sikhism (1.9 percent), Buddhism (0.8 percent) and Jainism (0.4 percent). The religious diversity of this modern democracy is a result of both the evolution of native religions as well as assimilation and social integration of religions brought by traders, travelers, immigrants, invaders and conquerors.

The dispersed Christians

Although Christians on the southern and western coast of India claim the apostolic traditions of St. Thomas and St. Bartholomew, the first recorded Catholic missionary was the Italian Franciscan, John of Montecorvino, in the 13th century. However, organised missions— and opposition to them—began with the arrival of the Portuguese in the 16th century, and the conquest of Goa in 1510, which began the history of India's colonisation.

Almost half of India's Christians live in five southern states – Tamil Nadu, Kerala, Karnataka, Andhra Pradesh and Telangana. The seven northeastern states and Goa together account for some 30 percent of Christians, with the remaining 20 percent dispersed across the northern states, and forming less than 1 percent of the population of most states.

In southern states, Goa and in the northeast, Christians generally do not face violent opposition, as they are politically and socially influential. These states have centuries of Christian tradition, unlike the northern Indian states, where Christian missions have gained strength only in the past century. In the tribal-dominated northeast, where Christian mission work is only a century old, Christianity is a majority religion in three states and a politically decisive power bloc.

Anti-conversion moves

Jain said that Hindu groups are determined to take action against missionaries who preach conversion. 'They [Christians] accuse us of persecution because we try to stop conversions [to Christianity]. They know we will not let this happen, so they accuse us.'

Jain's right-wing Vishva Hindu Parishad (VHP) now spearheads a national campaign called *ghar-vapasi* ('homecoming'), which is aimed at converting tribal and Dalit people back to Hinduism, which the VHP says is the spiritual 'home' of these people. The campaign can traced back to Dilip Singh Judeo, heir to the former Jashpur kingdom in central India, who began it some 20 years ago, alleging that Christian missionaries aim to convert poor and gullible tribal and Dalit people, luring them with money, material goods, and services such as education. Despite Dilip Singh Judeo's death in 2013, the VHP took up the approach as part of its political campaign, and several re-conversion events have been held across India, including in Kerala and Tamil Nadu.

The fierce opposition to missionary activities came to a tragic head when fanatics burnt to death Australian missionary Graham Staines and his two sons in January 1999 in Orissa. The BJP was in power at the time, and rights organisations like Human Rights Watch criticised the government's failure to protect religious minorities. Orissa State has seen several other attacks, including the murder of a Catholic priest following the Staines murders. However, anti-Christian riots in Kandhamal in 2007 and 2008, which left close to 100 Christians dead, and displaced some 50,000 more, remain the largest incidence of organised violence against Christians in the country.

In 1998, the BJP came to power in Gujarat, and, since then, that state has also witnessed tension. The following year, 1999,'began with an unprecedented hate campaign by Hindutva groups and culminated with ten days of nonstop violence against Christian tribals and the destruction of churches and Christian institutions' in the state, said Human Rights Watch.

But the opposition to religious conversion began even in pre-independence India, and continued in the national assembly that gathered to formulate the Indian constitution. The discussion to enact a national law banning 'forcible conversion' began 60 years ago, and it continues today with the BJP pressing for such legislation.

Although no national law against conversion exists, several states have laws that criminalise conversion if done without the permission of government officials. The laws, ironically named as 'freedom of religion' acts, carry jail terms and fines for attempting conversion through fraudulent means and allurements. Christian leaders say that missionary services offering education, health care and social welfare measures can be interpreted as allurements, and therefore pastors can be jailed.

'The anti-conversion laws target Muslims, and particularly Christians, and make it all but legitimate for any self-styled guardian of Hinduism to assault the religious minorities,' Dayal noted.

'It is a pity that all governments, without exception, since1950 have overlooked this, although the first prime minister, Jawaharlal Nehru, cautioned the nation against unleashing this monster,' Dayal added.

The Hindu response

Jain sees an international conspiracy against India and the BJP government in the Christian complaints of persecution. 'They [Christians] shout about persecution according to the policy and guidelines they receive at the international level. They work on the basis of these guidelines to tarnish the image of India,' he said.

He said in the hundreds of cases in which Christians accuse Hindu groups, investigations have not found any involvement by Hindus, adding that they have submitted a list of 52 cases of false accusations to the Federal Minorities Commission, including incidents of the alleged rape of nuns, and attacks on churches.

'They accused Hindus of raping a nun in West Bengal, but police arrested those responsible for the crime. They were Muslims from [neighboring] Bangladesh.'

But Church leaders in Madhya Pradesh and Chhattisgarh say the state machinery is put under pressure to act against Christians and in favor of Hindu fanatics. For example, Christy Abraham, head of India's National Christian Forum, said there have been more than 100 cases of violence against Christians in Madhya Pradesh since the BJP came to power in the state in 2003, but 'no one is arrested or punished.'

BJP parliamentarian Yogi Adityanath said, 'Sporadic incidents of violence' are projected out of proportion as the persecution of minorities. 'It is not proper to call it violence against minorities and Christians or Muslims,' he said.

'An impression has been created that the Modi government is anti-minority. This is not true,' he said, pointing out his party's alliance with Muslims in Kashmir, and partnerships in the Christian strongholds of Nagaland and Meghalaya.

Federal Culture Minister Mahesh Sharma has also denied allegations that the government is silent on atrocities against minorities, such as the lynching of the Muslim man in Uttar Pradesh. 'Who says the BJP leadership is silent on violence. From day one, I have been saying the lynching is a blot on our culture, and such incidents do not have a place in a civilised society. But if somebody says it was pre-planned, I don't agree with that. We take it as an accident, and an investigation is underway,' he said.

Looking ahead

Christian leaders pin their hopes on the majority of secular-minded Hindus in the country.

'The average Hindu is a decent citizen. The Hindu will not, in the final analysis, allow malevolent groups to claim leadership,' Dayal said. 'I think the sane Hindu will prevail. This is not a battle that Muslims and Christians have to fight. The Hindu has to fight to regain his birthright of freedom and world citizenship from the lunatics who were once the fringe but have now almost become the mainstream,' he said.

He added that people's movements are the lifeblood, the soul of a nation. 'They are the keepers of its conscience. In times of need, they can become the sinews and muscles of reform, and a bulwark against extremism.'

Howell agreed: 'Hinduism, by nature, has been a multicultural religion. The richness of Indian culture is its diversity; that is why it has sustained itself over centuries, because of its multiculturalism and acceptance. This is the standard Hindu position.'

Cardinal Cleem is was more assertive about the future of the Church when he addressed a gathering attended by Federal Home Minister Manohar Parrikar in May 2014. 'We will continue our work. What is our work? It is to spread the joy of the Gospel without offending anyone. There is no compromise on that,' he said.

Indonesia

By Katharina R Lestari assisted by Ryan Dagur

Syahidin Rajib and his family have lived in a shelter called Wisma Transitoon Lombok Island, West Nusa Tenggara Province, for more than nine years. They fled from their home at Ketapang Orong hamlet in the village of Gegerung, West Lombok District, after being accused by hardline Islamists of having tainted Islam.

On February 4, 2006, Islamists attacked houses in the hamlet belonging to followers of the Ahmadiyya sect, including Rajib's family. The machete-wielding mob threw stones at the houses and then set them alight with petrol. At least 24 homes were completely or partially burnt, while most of the Ahmadiyyas' personal possessions were either destroyed or stolen.

'Ahmadiyya followers are considered heretics by some people in our village,' said Rajib, a father of four children.

Twenty-nine families, comprising 116 Ahmadiyya followers, now live in Wisma Transito, with each family occupying a three-by-three meter space separated only by tarpaulins. The shelter has only13 toilets and one kitchen. They are safe here, but the life they lead is difficult. Nevertheless, Rajib said they still want to return home.

In the village of Jemundoin Sidoarjo District, East Java Province, more than 300Shia Muslims have taken refuge in a high-rise building called Puspa Agro since June 2013. They had previously fled to a sports complex in Sampang District following a Shia-Sunni conflict that broke out on August 26, 2012 on Madura. A mob of more than 500 Sunni Muslims attacked the Shia Muslims who were living in

Karang Gayam and Blu'uran villages, setting dozens of homes on fire. Two people died and 10 others were injured.

Among the displaced Shia Muslims is Iklil Al Milal. 'We don't feel at home here. We have our own villages. We always want to return home,' he said.

Other religious communities, including Protestants and Catholics, living in the predominantly Muslim country, find themselves struggling to comply with a contentious decree on places of worship.

The congregations of the Christian Church in Indonesia, known as GKI Yasmin, in Bogor, and the Batak Protestant Church, known as HKBP Filadelfia, in the Islamic stronghold of Bekasi, both in West Java Province, have held Sunday services twice a month in front of the Presidential Palace in Jakarta since February 2012, after being banned from using their own churches by the local authorities. On September 27, 2015, they held their 100th Sunday service.

The GKI Yasmin congregation has been banned from using its church because of alleged irregularities regarding the decree. A Supreme Court ruling, which has been backed by the ombudsman, stating that the congregation has the right to worship in the church, has been ignored by the local mayor. Protestants from HKBP Filadelfia are embroiled in a similar case.

'The two churches are valid. But they are still illegally sealed by the Bogor and Bekasi authorities, without any corrections from the central government under the leadership of former president Susilo Bambang Yudhoyono and current president Joko Widodo. How long should we face this?' asked Bona Sigalingging, a spokesman for GKI Yasmin.

Diversity

Persecution and discrimination against religious minorities isn't a new thing in the world's largest archipelago country. With more than 17,000 islands, there are a number of religious groups. Yet, the 1965 blasphemy law, enacted under the first president, Sukarno, says that the state has six main religions—Buddhism, Catholicism, Confucianism, Hinduism, Islam and Protestantism.

'The government's interpretation is that it only serves the six religions,' said Ahmad Suaedy, executive director of the Jakarta-based Wahid Institute.

According to the 2010 census, the most recent conducted by the Central Board of Statistics, Indonesia had a total population of 237.6 million people that year. In 2015, the board projected a total population of 284.8 million people by the time of the next census.

In the census – which is conducted once a decade—207.2 million Indonesians, or 87.2 percent of the population, identified themselves as Muslim. Around 16.5 million identified as Protestant, 6.9 million Catholic, 4 million Hindu, 1.7 million Buddhist, and 117,000 Confucian. The remainder were followers of smaller religions and traditional beliefs.

West Java Province had the largest Muslim population, with 41.8 million people. East Java and Central Java provinces followed, with 36.1 and 31.3 million people, respectively

Protestants were the majority group in North Sumatra Province, with3.5 million adherents. East Nusa Tenggara and North Sulawesi provinces ranked second and third, with 1.6 and 1.4 million, respectively.

The province with the largest Catholic population was East Nusa Tenggara, with 2.5 million adherents. West Kalimantan Province followed, with 1 million. The third largest Catholic population was in North Sumatra Province, with 516,000.

Hindus form a major group in Bali Province, with had 3.2 million adherents. West Nusa Tenggara and Lampung provinces also have large Hindu populations, with 118,000 and 114,000 adherents, respectively.

Buddhists are concentrated in Jakarta, North Sumatra and West Kalimantan provinces. In Jakarta, there were 318,000 Buddhists. North Sumatra and West Kalimantan provinces were home to 304,000 and 238,000 Buddhists, respectively.

In Bangka-Belitung Islands Province, Confucians were the majority group, with 40,000 adherents. West Kalimantan and West Java provinces followed, with 30,000 and 15,000, respectively.

Followers of smaller religions, including Shia and Ahmadiyya Muslims, as well as more than 200 traditional beliefs, can also be found in Indonesia.

The New York-based Human Rights Watch's 2013 report entitled *In Religion's Name: Abuses Against Religious Minorities in Indonesia* quotes the All-Indonesian Assembly of Alhulbayt Associations, a national Shia organisation established in 2000, as saying that there were around 2.5 million Shia Muslims in 2009. Another Shia organisation that emerged in 2010, Ahlul Bait Indonesia, said most Shia Muslims live in East Java and West Java provinces.

The Ahmadiyya sect was founded by Mirza Ghulam Ahmad in 1889, and its first missionaries arrived in Sumatra in 1925. A year later, the first Ahmadiyya mosque was established in Padang, West Sumatra Province. In 1953, the Indonesian Ahmadiyya Congregation, the sect's national organization, was legally registered in Jakarta.

Human Rights Watch reported that there are no statistics on the number of Ahmadiyya followers in Indonesia. However, former religious affairs minister, Suryadharma Ali, who has said that the Ahmadiyya sect should be banned, estimated that it has 50,000 members in the country, denying media reports that it has 400,000 members.

Most Muslims in Indonesia are Sunni, and most of those belong to either of two large organisations, namely Nahdlatul Ulama and Muhammadiyah.

Nahdlatul Ulama, established in 1926 in Jombang District of East Java Province, operates thousands of *pesantren,* or Islamic boarding schools, mostly on Java. This organisation claims to have 40 to 50 million members, making it the largest Islamic organisation in the country.

Muhammadiyah, which was established in 1912 in Yogyakarta Province, is a reformist Islamic movement that has set up schools and hospitals, and works to purify the teaching of Islam. It is the second-largest Islamic organisation in the country.

Even though the government serves only the six main religions, Religious Affairs Minister Lukman Hakim Saifuddin said in August 2014 that Baha'i should also be added to the list, noting that Baha'i followers are scattered across the country, but in small numbers, including in Banyuwangi District (220 followers), Surabaya (98 followers) and Malang (30 followers) (all in East Java Province), Jakarta Province (100 followers), Medan in North Sumatra Province

(100 followers), Palopo in South Sulawesi Province (80 followers) and Bandung in West Java Province (50 followers).

The Baha'ifaithemerged in what is now Iran in the 19th century, and its roots in Indonesia can be traced back to the 1920s.It was outlawed in the country from 1962, until former president Abdurrahman Wahid lifted the ban in 2000.

In addition to its religious diversity, Indonesia is also rich in ethnicity. According to the last census, the country is home to 1,128 ethnic groups.

Human Rights Watch's report said that ethnicity is an important factor in, and remains closely intertwined with, religion, with different ethnic groups practicing different faiths.

The ten largest ethnic groups are Javanese (83.8 million), Sundanese (30.9 million), Malay (6.9 million), Madurese (6.7 million), Batak (6.0 million), Minangkabau (5.5 million), Betawi (5.0 million), Buginese (5.0 million), Bantenese (4.1 million) and Banjarese (3.5 million).

The Javanese, Sundanese, Malay and Madurese are predominantly Sunni Muslim, while the Batakare majority Christian.

This portrait of diversity is in accordance with the national motto *Bhinneka Tunggal Ika* ('Unity in Diversity'), which has long been upheld by the powers that be. However, the persecution of, and discrimination against, religious minorities will likely continue.

'We are plural in terms of religion and ethnicity. Conflicts will always be there. So the effort to maintain [pluralism] needs the government to play a role,' said Bonar Tigor Naipospos, deputy director of the Jakarta-based Setara Institute for Democracy and Peace.

Government failure

When Indonesia achieved independence on August 17,1945, the first president, Sukarno, declared his vision for the 1945 constitution called Pancasila (Five principles). Enshrined in the preamble of the constitution, this stipulates the belief in one God, a just and civilised society, a united Indonesia, democracy guided by consensus, and social justice for all.

The constitution explicitly promises the right to religious freedom, under Article 29(2), which stipulates that 'the state guarantees each and every citizen the freedom of religion and of worship in accordance with his religion and belief.'

However, since then, a number of regulations have led to persecution and discrimination against religious minorities.

'There is the 2006 joint ministerial decree on places of worship, the 1965 blasphemy law, and the sharia-based regulations,' said Naipospos.

The decree is an amendment of the 1969 regulation, and was issued by the Religious Affairs and Home Affairs ministries. It lays out onerous requirements, including that Church officials must provide a list of names and signatures of 90 worshippers, and have signed support from at least 60 local residents and approval from the village head before they can build a church.

Both Protestants and Catholics are victimised by the decree.

On August 10, 2015, more than a thousand Sunni Muslims staged a rally in front of the mayor's office in Bekasi. They urged the local authorities to revoke a building permit officially obtained a few weeks earlier by St Clara Parish. The parish, which bought a 6,500-square meter plot of land in 2000, obtained the building permit on July 28, 2015 after meeting the requirements stipulated in the decree, as well as a 2006 mayoral regulation on the construction of places of worship.

'We have gone through all the procedures. All administrative processes are done,' said Rasniu Pasaribu, a Church secretary in the parish, which was established in 1996 and currently ministers to 2,498 families or 9,422 Catholics.

London-based Amnesty International's 2014 report entitled *Prosecuting Beliefs: Indonesia's Blasphemy Laws* said that Indonesia's blasphemy law covers two types of blasphemous act: deviation from one of the six main religions, and defamation of one of those religions, as stipulated in articles 1 and 4.

Article 1 states:'Every individual is prohibited in public from intentionally conveying, endorsing or attempting to gain public support in the interpretation of a certain religion embraced by the people of Indonesia, or undertaking religious-based activities that resemble the religious activities of the religion in question, where such interpretation and activities are in deviation of the basic teachings of the religion.'

Article 4 stipulates: 'A maximum term of imprisonment of five years shall be imposed on whosoever in public deliberately expresses their feelings or engages in action that: (a) in principle is hostile and considered as abuse or defamation of a religion embraced in Indonesia, and (b) has the intention that a person should not practice any religion at all that is based on belief in Almighty God.'

Amnesty's report also states that the blasphemy law's provisions have inspired the use of similar provisions in more recently enacted laws. At least two laws have been used to prosecute people accused of defaming religion, namely the 2008 law on electronic information and transactions, and the 2002 law on the protection of children.

'If Indonesia wants to be a democratic state, annul the blasphemy law. The joint ministerial decree is a consensus indeed, but in practice there are many holes misused by intolerant groups to attack [other religious groups],' said Naipospos.

The Setara Institute records around 150 sharia-based regulations in more than 70 regions in Indonesia. In Aceh Province, for example, sharia law began to be implemented in 2001,with the aim of supporting the local people. A year later, the province issued a by-law on the implementation of sharia law. In 2003, several by-laws on alcohol, gambling and seclusion were issued.

Meanwhile, *QanunHukumJinayat*, the Islamic criminal code, started to be implemented in September 2015 – one year after its passage by the Aceh legislative council.

'We have the support of Acehnese society because we have a long history of the implementation of sharia in the Aceh kingdom,' said Syahrizal Abbas, head of Aceh Province's Islamic Sharia Agency. 'Acehnese society follows the ideology of Islam. We have about a 98 percent Muslim population.'

In June 2008, the religious affairs and home affairs ministers, and the attorney-general, issued an anti-Ahmadiyya joint decree. According to Human Rights Watch's report, the decree has opened the door for governors, mayors and district heads to write their own anti-Ahmadiyya decrees. The Indonesian Ahmadiyya Congregation reported in 2011 that five provinces—Banten, East Java, West Java, West Sumatra and South Sulawesi—and 22 municipalities and districts in Indonesia had issued anti-Ahmadiyya regulations.

According to Andreas Harsono, an Indonesian researcher at Amnesty, the persecution and discrimination of religious minorities wasgenerally created under the leadership of former president Yudhoyono.

Yudhoyono, a retired general, took office in October 2004, and secured a second term in 2009. Indonesian law allows only two consecutive presidential terms.

'The government led by Yudhoyono had a hint of sectarianism. What is the proof? The number of violent incidents continued to increase under his leadership, and there were no strict actions against perpetrators,' said Harsono.

The Setara Instituterecorded216 cases of violent attacks on religious minorities in 2010, 244 cases in 2011, and 264 cases in 2012. Meanwhile, the Wahid Institute recorded 92 violations of religious freedom, and 184 incidents of religious intolerance in 2011, up from 64 violations and 134 incidents of intolerance in 2010.

The Setara Institute categorises two main perpetrators or actors: the state and civilians. Violent acts committed by the state include direct action (by commission), ignorance (by omission) and issuance of discriminative regulations (by rule of law or the judiciary), while those committed by civilians included crimes and incidents of intolerance.

'Under the leadership of Yudhoyono, there were also discriminatory regulations. Let's take the joint ministerial decree on places of worship. Yudhoyono also switched the concept of religious freedom into religious harmony,' said Harsono.

Besides laying out onerous requirements, the decree also requires local governments to set up an Interfaith Harmony Forum in each province, district or town, aimed at building, maintaining and empowering the faithful, so as to create interfaith harmony and prosperity.

The composition of the local forum should mirror the composition of believers in the province, district or town, meaning that a predominantly Muslim area may have significantly more Muslim members than Christians, and vice versa.

The forum in each district or town has the responsibility to offer written recommendations for the establishment of places of worship.

'But then the forums started to deal with other issues such as the renovation of places of worship, religious-based conflicts and so on. It is a source of problems, as it is where the principle of majority and minority is highlighted. This is against the 1945 constitution,' said Harsono. 'I see that the government is the perpetrator of persecution.'

Fundamentalist groups

Fundamentalist groups emerged in Indonesia during the period of Dutch colonialism, according to Harsono.

'Under the leadership of Yudhoyono, however, they were given fresh impetus. Yudhoyono built a coalition with them. For example, after being elected as president in 2004, he said at a congress of the Indonesian Ulema Council that the government would listen to the council's fatwa [Islamic edict],' he said.

Yudhoyono gave the legitimacy of truth towards the council's interpretation of Islamic teachings.

'So the council becamevery powerful under Yudhoyono in terms of the interpretation of Islamic teachings,' said Suaedy of the Wahid Institute.

The Ulema Council'swebsite lists a number of Islamic edicts, including a fatwa about Ahmadiyya. This fatwa was first issued during the council's national congress in 1980, when the council deemed that the Ahmadiyya group wasn't part of the Islamic faith, and that its followers were infidels. During a national congress in July 2005, the council renewed the fatwa, urging the government to ban and disband the community, and stop all of its activities.

Thisfatwa has often led fundamentalist groups such as the Islamic Defenders Front (FPI) to persecute Ahmadiyya followers. In June 2015, for example, local residents in Bukit Duri, south Jakarta, and members of FPI,blocked the entrance of the small An-Nur mosque belonging to Ahmadiyya followers, with a protest rally.

'FPI needs to take action against violations emerging in society. There are two kinds of violation: legal and ethical violations. What followers of Ahmadiyya and Shia do, as well as other heretical sects, is an ethical violation,' said Habib Muhsin bin Ahmad Al-Attas, who heads FPI.

'If we are called fundamentalists, upholding our religion, yes, we are fundamentalists. A fundamentalist must obey his religion,' he added, saying that FPI aims at enforcing Islamic religious teachings.

In Naipospos' view, fundamentalist groups in Indonesia generally have only one purpose, namely creating an Islamic state with sharia-based regulations.

'The approach is different though. Jihadists use violence to reach their goal. For them, if they can gain power, they can control other groups. Other groups slowly implement sharia-based regulations at the low level. At the national level, they try to put Islamic law, covering such things as pornography law, into practice,' he said.

However, Slamet Effendy Yusuf, deputy chairman of Nahdlatul Ulama, said that fundamentalists in transnational groups are generally influenced by foreigners. 'They are small, and their funding must have something to do with foreign parties supporting them,' he said.

The good thing is that the country has the founding principles of Pancasila.

'This is the first pillar, so that fundamentalist groups won't succeed easily in their goals,' Naipospos said, adding that the two largest Islamic organisations also serve as other pillars.

Nahdlatul Ulama embarked on a campaign to promote Islam Nusantara (Islam of the Archipelago) in August 2015, aimed at combating extremism and reinforcing the long-held ideal of a pluralistic identity. Islam Nusantara embraces the idea of a Muslim-majority nation with moderate views and religious tolerance.

'For Nahdlatul Ulama, the Unitary State of the Republic of Indonesia is a fixed goal. It's final. Nahdlatul Ulama sees contextualisation as a foundation,' Yusuf said.

In March 2015, the Setara Institute conducted a survey involving 684 students from 114 senior high schools in Jakarta and Bandung, capital of West Java Province. Jakarta and Bandung were chosen because Jakarta is a barometer of other cities in the country, while Bandung has seen a high incidence of religious intolerance. The survey found that 515 students, or 75.3 percent of those surveyed, were aware of the Islamic State (IS) movement in Syria, Iraq and other places in the Middle East and Africa. Of this number, 7.2 percent actually agreed with the actions and atrocities committed by IS in Syria and Iraq.

The survey also revealed that a large number of the students were in favor of banning or limiting the activities of Ahmadiyya and Shia followers in Indonesia, because they are not in line with Sunni doctrine.

Homework

In Indonesia, there are still many legal edicts that can lead to persecution and discrimination against religious minorities.

'It's true, there are many problematic regulations seen as creating persecution and discrimination against certain religious communities. These have got our attention,' said Nur Syam, secretary-general of the Religious Affairs Ministry.

In order to deal with the issue, in February 2015 the government established a coordinating forum led by the Religious Affairs and Home Affairs ministries. It was formed as a response to, and part of the government's efforts, to find a solution to issues related to the freedom of worship or religion.

The government now prioritises six issues, namely the conflict between Sunni and Shia Muslims, the persecution and discrimination faced by Ahmadiyya followers, the building permit for the GKI Yasmin congregation, the movement to fight terrorism, the existence of local religions, and the 'protection' of all religions.

'Obviously, the government has the commitment,' Syam said, adding that the administration will rethink regulations in accordance with today's context, and with input from different parties.

'It's possible [for the government to review regulations]. The space is wide open,' Syam added.

However, the National Commission on Human Rights' special rapporteur on religious freedom recently listed challenges faced by the government.

'Not all state agencies have an understanding of the right to religion or belief. Many state agencies in local areas still can't differentiate between the right to religion or belief that can't be limited, and the rights that can be limited,' said Imdadun Rahmat in a statement issued in July 2015.

Leaders are at the core of the problem, according to some critics.

'Leaders are not strong enough to implement the existing regulations. The problem right now is law enforcement,' said Father Antonius Benny Susetyo, who is former executive secretary of the Commission for Ecumenical and Inter-religious Affairs of the Indonesian Bishops' Conference, and now secretary of the Setara Institute's National Council.

There is also external pressure, as Indonesia plays an increasingly significant role in the world.

'They see Islam in Indonesia as a successful religion, as it can manifest moderation. They also hope that Islam in Indonesia can be an ideal model,' said Naipospos.

'If Islam in Indonesia fails, the effect on other countries will be very bad. Islam in Indonesia has a different history compared to that in the Middle East and even neighboring countries,' Naipospos added, saying that Islam in Indonesia is open, moderate and tolerant.

'There are many sects that adapt to the local cultures, such as Nahdlatul Ulama and Muhammadiyah,' said Harsono—which fosters the belief that Indonesia will not see the kind of conflict that has occurred in places like Afghanistan.

Still, the government has much to do to improve religious tolerance in the country.

'In general, there are still many things to improve. The issue of violence and the weakness of the government are important to note,' Harsono added.

Pakistan

In September 2014, Punjab Cardiology Hospital, Lahore, took out an advertisement in local newspapers for sanitation jobs, stating that 'Only non-Muslims who belong to minorities will be accommodated.' The advertisement drew immediate flak from minority rights campaigners, who found it offensive, degrading and a continuation of the marginalisation of non-Muslims in Pakistan.

There action from the activists found some space in news publications, prompting the hospital administration to issue a corrigendum two weeks later, which said that both Muslims and non-Muslims were eligible to submit applications for sanitation jobs.

This was not the first time that a public entity had reserved sanitation work for non-Muslims and, as things stand, it won't be the last.

Pakistan came into existence in the name of Islam after Muslims of the Indian sub-continent called for a separate homeland, pleading that there was nothing in common between them and Hindus. Their dream materialised in 1947, and in his first address to the Constituent Assembly of Pakistan, Muhammad Ali Jinnah, the nation's founder, presented his vision for the newly-born state.

'We should begin to work in that spirit, and in the course of time, all these angularities of the majority and minority communities, the Hindu community and the Muslim community, because even as regards Muslims you have Pathans, Punjabis, Shias, Sunnis and so on, and among the Hindus you have Brahmins, Vashnavas, Khatris, also Bengalis, Madrasis and so on, will vanish.

'Indeed, if you ask me, this has been the biggest hindrance in the way of India to attain freedom and independence, and but for this we would have been free people long, long ago. No power can hold another nation, and especially a nation of 400 million souls in subjection; nobody could have conquered you, and even if it had happened, nobody could have continued a hold on you for any length of time, but for this. Therefore, we must learn a lesson from this.

'You are free; you are free to go to your temples, you are free to go to your mosques or to any other place of worship in this state of Pakistan. You may belong to any religion or caste or creed that has nothing to do with the business of the state.

'As you know, history shows that in England, conditions, some time ago, were much worse than those prevailing in India today. The Roman Catholics and the Protestants persecuted each other. Even now there are some states in existence where there are discriminations made, and bars imposed, against a particular class.

'Thank God, we are not starting in those days. We are starting in days where there is no discrimination, no distinction between one community and another, no discrimination between one caste or creed and another. We are starting with this fundamental principle that we are all citizens and equal citizens of one state. The people of England in course of time had to face the realities of the situation, and had to discharge the responsibilities and burdens placed upon them by the government of their country, and they went through that fire, step by step. Today, you might say with justice that Roman Catholics and Protestants do not exist; what exists now is that every man is a citizen, an equal citizen of Great Britain, and they are all members of the nation.

'Now I think we should keep that in front of us as our ideal, and you will find that in the course of time, Hindus will cease to be Hindus, and Muslims will cease to be Muslims, not in the religious sense, because that is the personal faith of each individual, but in the political sense, as citizens of the state.

'I can look forward to Pakistan becoming one of the greatest nations of the world,' he concluded.

Jinnah's vision indeed could have made Pakistan one of the greatest nations, but little did he know what was to come after his demise.

A country that was founded by a Shia Muslim was virtually turned into a living hell for the minority Shia who, along with Christians, Hindus and Ahmadis, became the prime target of Sunni extremists.

Ahmadis were constitutionally declared non-Muslims; Christians and Hindus were made to suffer from harsh blasphemy laws; while Shias were regarded as 'kafirs,' or infidels.

Discriminatory laws, the state's patronage of militant groups, deep-rooted intolerance and chronic ignorance gave rise to incidents of persecution in Pakistan.

In May 2015, the US Commission on International Religious Freedom (USCIRF) pointed out that Pakistan topped the list of countries that jailed citizens for allegedly attacking religion. The USCIRF estimates the Shia population at between 10 and 12 percent of Pakistan's total, among whom around 900,000 are Ismailis, which is a sect that pays tribute to its living spiritual leader, the Aga Khan. It also lists the number of Christians at 2.09 million; Ahmadis at 286,000; Hindus at 1.03 million; Parsis, Buddhists and Sikhs at 20,000 each; and Baha'is at 50,000 to100,000.

Who are Pakistan's minorities?

Christians

Christians are the most persecuted religious minority in Pakistan, and in recent years have suffered deadly terrorist attacks that have left hundreds of them dead. In Lahore in March 2015, churches were attacked, resulting in the deaths of over a dozen people, and sparking riots in the city that lasted for three days.

But more than terrorism, Christian leaders have long campaigned against the misuse of blasphemy laws, which have led to many incidents of mob violence. The law mandates that any 'blasphemies' against the Koran carry the death sentence.

Rights campaigner say that the laws are often used by people to settle personal scores and to instila sense of terror. A prime example of this was the recent murder of Shama Bibi and her husband Sajjad Masih in Kot Radha Kishan, Punjab. On November 4, 2015 the Christian couple was beaten to death and then burned by an angry mob that had been told that the couple had desecrated a copy of the Koran. Local clerics used loudspeakers to incite the mob.

The victims were working as bonded laborers at a brick kiln. It was reported that the couple knew that they were in danger before the attack, and went to the kiln owner to seek permission to leave.

Instead, he locked them in a room and told them that they could not leave until they had cleared their debt. The mob found them there, beat them to death with bricks and shovels, and then burned their bodies in a kiln. Shama was expecting her fifth child. The suspects were apprehended after a few days.

In an earlier case in November 2010, Asia Bibi was sentenced to death by hanging for 'blasphemy'; the sentence has to be upheld in a higher court before she can be executed.

Anti-Ahmadi mullahs are in close contact with so-called jihadi outfits who consider terrorism a fair tactic in national and international politics. Thus, the carnage in two Ahmadiyya mosques in Lahore on May 28, 2010 that resulted in 86 deaths. This act was allegedly sponsored by End of Prophet hood clerics, and was carried out by terrorists trained and hired out by some militant group in the Federally Administered Tribal Areas (FATA).

In March 2011, Shahbaz Bhatti, the federal minister for minority affairs, was murdered by Islamist gunmen after he spoke out against Pakistan's blasphemy laws. The Catholic Church in Pakistan requested that Pope Benedict declare him a martyr.

In August 2012, Rimsha Masih, a Christian girl, variously reportedly as 11 or 14 years old, and an illiterate with mental disabilities, was accused of blasphemy for burning pages from a book containing koranic verses. The allegation came from a Muslim cleric who has subsequently been accused by the police of framing the girl. The girl, and later the cleric, were both arrested and released on bail.

Thousands seek asylum

Activists and members of the Christian community say that around 5,000 Christians have fled the country because of threats, persecution and lack of security. Many of them have escaped to Thailand and Sri Lanka, where they have applied for asylum. Some representatives of the Christian community in Thailand say they have around 10,000 registered Pakistani asylum seekers.

Hindus

Forced conversion to Islam has long been the main concern for Hindus in Pakistan. According to Hindu leaders, Hindu girls, most of them underage, are kidnapped, forcibly converted and then married to Muslim men in Sindh.

Doctor Ramesh Kumar Vankwani, head of the Pakistan Hindu Council, said that hundreds of girls are forcefully converted every year, prompting some Hindus to migrate to India.

'Around 5,000 Hindus migrate from Pakistan to India every year due to religious persecution,' he said, adding that the government had failed in its duty to protect Hindus from attacks, and to prevent forced conversions.

The Hindu community has long been irked by the lack of codified Hindu personal laws, particularly a Hindu marriage law. A Hindu Marriage Bill was tabled in the parliament in 2011, but it has still not been passed.

The Supreme Court of Pakistan has also directed the government to take measures to register Hindu marriages. Muslims and Christians can obtain marriage certificates from the government, but Hindus have no documentary proof of their marriage.

Once passed, the Hindu Marriage Act would offer the Hindu community some protection against forced conversion and harassment by police. It would also enable them to settle other issues such as divorce and inheritance.

Persecution of Ahmadis in Pakistan

The Ahmadiyya Muslim Jama'at was formed in Qadian, India in 1889 by Hadhrat Mirza Ghulam Ahmad, but Ahmadis in Pakistan have faced many problems since a 1974 constitutional amendment declared them non-Muslim.

Saleedud Din, spokesman of the Ahamdi community in Pakistan, said the group rejects all forms of terrorism, and is opposed to the concept of violence to promote religion—the present-day concept of jihad. He said Ahmadis are targeted because they are vehemently opposed to this interpretation of jihad.

'In Pakistan and some other Muslim countries, mullahs, politicians and generals in power have cooperated with one another to suppress and persecute the community,' he said.

In 1974, Zulfikar Ali Bhutto, the then-prime minister of Pakistan, found it politically advantageous to impose non-Muslim status on Ahmadis, which opened the door for the persecution of the community. Ten years later, in 1984, General Zia-ul-Haq promulgated Ordinance XX, which effectively bans the Ahmadiyya faith and has adversely affected the everyday life of Ahmadis. This piece of legislation made it a criminal offense punishable by three years' imprisonment and an unlimited fine for anyone who practiced, propagated or even proclaimed the faith.

Yahanan Friedmann, a research scholar, in his book *Prophecy Continuous* (University of California Press, 1989),writes: 'The ordinance promulgated by the president on April 26, 1984 goes a long way to accepting the most extreme anti-Ahmadi demands, and transforms much of the daily life of the community into a criminal offense.'

This law breaks the constitutional guarantee provided by Article 20 on freedom of religion; it blatantly violates Article 18 of the Universal Declaration of Human Rights; goes against the spirit of the United Nations Charter; and is an obvious outrage against the UN General Assembly's Declaration on the Elimination of All Forms of Intolerance and Discrimination based on Religion or Belief.

The UN Sub-Commission on the Prevention of Discrimination and Protection of Minorities has expressed its 'grave concern' at the promulgation of this ordinance, and requested that the UN Commission on Human Rights (UNHRC)call on the government of Pakistan to repeal it (E/CN.4/Sub.2/1985/L.42 of August 27, 1985). It is nevertheless relentlessly applied.

As a result, since 1984, hundreds of Ahmadis have been murdered because of their faith, and the authorities have not prosecuted even 5 percent of the assailants.

In October 2005, eight Ahmadis were killed and 20 wounded when religious zealots sprayed bullets at worshippers in an Ahmadiyya mosque at Mong, Mandi Bahauddin District. The killers were later arrested but freed after a court trial.

Both the state and clerics have targeted Ahmadiyya mosques. Twenty-two mosques have been demolished, 28 sealed by the authorities, 12 set on fire and 15 have been forcibly occupied since 1984.

In June 2008, the authorities in Azad Kashmir blew up an Ahmadiyya mosque that was under construction in Kotli District. On January 14, 2010 the authorities in the Punjab handed over an Ahmadiyya mosque in Ahmad Nagar to non-Ahmadis, although it was built by Ahmadis on land owned by an Ahmadi, and had been under Ahmadiyya management for 20years.

The many problems that Ahmadis in Pakistan have faced since the 1974 constitutional amendment declared them non-Muslim continued in 2014, when 86 Ahmadi worshipers were slain in two mosques in Lahore, Punjab, where the Pakistan Muslim League (PML)-(N) is in power.

The law has been interpreted and applied maliciously all over Pakistan, often out of all context. For instance, bodies of Ahmadi dead have been disinterred from public graveyards, despite the fact that there is no provision in the law for this act.

Under the law, Ahmadis cannot vote unless they do so as 'non-Muslims.'During his tenure, former president General Pervez Musharraf ostensibly reinstated the Joint Electorate system, to the acclaim of the international community, but a few days later he withdrew from this position and ordered a separate 'supplementary list,' only for Ahmadis, through Chief Executive Order No. 15 of 2002.

The application form for voters' registration has now been so maliciously and cunningly devised by the government that Ahmadis are unable to register as voters. Hence, in the 2008 elections, Ahmadis were conspicuous for having been denied the right to exercise their vote.

In the town of Rabwah, which serves as the headquarters for the community, and where 95 percent of the residents are Ahmadi, the local councils do not have even a single Ahmadi representative. Ahmadis have no say in the affairs of the local union councils. As a consequence, essential civic services like water supply, roads and sewage are in a deplorable state in this town of 60,000.

Through Ordinance XX, which was later enacted as law, a ban was imposed on all Ahmadiyya publications. Even the community's daily newspaper was put out of print. The ban on the daily remained in force for almost four years. Even now the Ahmadiyya press faces many obstacles. It is not allowed to use words like 'amen' or '*inshallah*' (God willing) or to reprint koranicverses. On the other hand, the vernacular press in Pakistan is given a free hand to print the most provocative and insulting views and fabrications against Ahmadis.

Ahmadis' right to peaceful religious assembly has been severely curtailed. The annual convention of the community in Rabwah has been prevented from being held since 1984, while non-Ahmadis, with the help of the government, are able to hold numerous highly slanderous open-air conferences every year in Rabwah, causing disquiet and discomfort to its residents. The government changed the name of Rabwah to Chenab Nagar in 1999, against the wishes of its residents.

In May 2008, Ahmadis wanted to celebrate the centenary of the Ahmadiyya Khilafat(a pan-Islamic, political protest campaign launched by Muslims in British India to influence the British government), but the police prohibited them from doing so. Some years ago the police even tried to arrest the entire population of the town. The authorities have also prohibited community sports, rallies and celebrations at all levels.

The authorities have even prohibited Rabwah town from hosting the Junior National Basketball Championship. In 2008, the government of the Punjab sponsored an 'End of the Prophet hood' conference in the provincial capital. Ahmadi schoolchildren were arrested by the Punjab police under the blasphemy law and were kept behind bars for approximately six months before their release on bail. The mullah and unscrupulous authorities continue to implement bad laws.

In education, Ahmadi students encounter unabashed prejudice in public institutions of higher learning, and in professional education. Events that occurred in the Punjab Medical College, Faisalabad in June and July 2008 are public knowledge. The principal rusticated all 23 male and female Ahmadi students. With great difficulty, some, but not all, of these students, were reinstated, but some had to switch to other colleges.

This deplorable law (Ordinance XX) continues to be applied extensively and heedlessly. Violations of Ahmadis' religious freedoms are systematic, ongoing and egregious. To date, more than 3,500 criminal cases have been registered against Ahmadis throughout Pakistan under the provisions of the anti-Ahmadiyya and other religious laws like the blasphemy laws. In 2014, 67 Ahmadis faced fresh charges.

Ahmadis charged under a blasphemy clause, PPC 295-A, have also been prosecuted in anti-terrorism courts, although it is they who suffer from terrorism at the hands of the state.

For two or three decades now, the Ahmadiyya community in Pakistan has experienced prolific and persistent hate propaganda from the vernacular print media. The electronic media has joined this ugly campaign somewhat recently. News reports, op-eds and comments against Ahmadis are often grossly false, provocative and orchestrated.

The law does not allow Ahmadis to explain their position in public (as it is deemed to be proselytising), but the authorities, in the name of freedom of the press and the media, do not warn hate-mongers to stop their rancor. In 2014, referring to the Ahmadiyya situation in Pakistan, the International Humanist and Ethical Union conveyed this message to the UNHRC: 'Need we remind the Council and the government of Pakistan that it was government and media support for expressions of hatred that led to the Nazi Holocaust and the genocide in Rwanda.'

Regrettably, the judiciary provides little relief for the persecuted community. Lower courts generally, and higher courts often, interpret the anti-Ahmadi laws very harshly. Even the Supreme Court has given the senseless inference, in 1993, that an Ahmadi who displays any commitment to the creed commits blasphemy against the Holy Prophet.

With such a loose definition of 'blasphemy' and the attitude of the apex court, hundreds of Ahmadis have been exposed to the mischief of the blasphemy law, which now prescribes nothing but death for its victims. Two hundred and ninety-eight Ahmadis have faced trumped-up charges under the blasphemy law to date. In this environment, one is not surprised that for the last quarter century there has not been a single day when an Ahmadi was not in prison for the reason of his or her faith.

Since the death of General Zia in 1988, no government, democratic or military, has provided any relief to the Ahmadis. General Musharraf took over the government in 1999, but despite his apparent liberalism and rhetoric about enlightened moderation, he did nothing to halt the persecution of Ahmadis by the state. Instead, the general placated the mullahs and reintroduced the entry column on religion in new machine-readable Pakistani passports. In addition, the application form for passports obligates a Muslim citizen to deny the veracity of the founder of the Ahmadi community, and to affirm his faith in the absolute end of Prophethood.

Pakistan still adopts a medieval approach in its treatment of Ahmadis. They continue to face severe discrimination and persecution under the present 'democratic' government, in every sphere of public and civil life. The severity of state-supported persecution has forced thousands of Ahmadis to flee the country and seek shelter abroad. The Human Rights Commission of Pakistan (HRCP) candidly wrote in its annual report: 'Ahmadis faced the worst discrimination and remained effectively disenfranchised. The HRCP continued to demand that the Joint Electorate be fully restored.' International human rights organisations like Amnesty International and the USCIRF have often reported on the plight of Ahmadis in Pakistan, but the situation has worsened since 2008.

In recent months, more Ahmadis have been murdered, places of worship have been desecrated, criminal cases have been registered against groups of Ahmadis on religious grounds, and various Ahmadi communities have suffered violence and oppression. Topics such as 'blood, jihad and the duty to kill' have been discussed in popular electronic media in the Ahmadiyya context, and target killings of Ahmadi leaders have taken place. In 2014, during the great flood disaster in the country, Ahmadis were denied shelter by the authorities in flood-affected areas in southern Punjab.

Updated statistics of police cases registered against Ahmadis on religious grounds, in Pakistan(From April 1984 to September 30, 2015)

No.	Description of case	Total number of cases
1	Number of Ahmadis arrested for displaying Kalima, i.e. 'There is none worthy of worship except Allah, Muhammad is the Messenger of Allah.'	765
2	Number of Ahmadis arrested for calling Azan, the call to prayers.	38
3	Number of Ahmadis arrested for 'posing'as Muslims.	447
4	Number of Ahmadis arrested for using Islamic epithets.	161
5	Number of Ahmadis arrested for offering prayers.	93
6	Number of Ahmadis arrested for preaching.	796
7	Number of Ahmadis arrested for celebrating the Ahmadiyya centenary in 1989.	27
8	Number of Ahmadis arrested for celebrating the 100-years anniversary of the eclipses of the sun and moon that occurred in 1894 as a sign of the Promised Mahdi, i.e. founder of the Ahmadiyya community.	50
9	Number of Ahmadis arrested for distributing a pamphlet *EkHarf-e-Nasihana* (‹A Word of Advice›) commenting upon the anti-Ahmadiyya Ordinance XX.	27
10	Number of Ahmadis arrested for distributing a pamphlet 'Mubahala' (a challenge to opponents to a prayer duel)	148

Sikhs

Although Pakistan is the birthplace of Guru Nanak, the founder of Sikhism, life for the Sikh community, especially in restive Khyber Pakhtunkhwa, is nothing but an ordeal. Sikhs are faced with kidnappings for ransom, and target killings by militants, according to the HRCP annual report. Kidnappers often set the ransom so high that the families of victims are unable to pay, and the abducted victims are killed.

A lot of Sikhs have fled to safety in places like Rawalpindi, so that they can run their businesses in a relatively secure environment. Frustrated by the government's failure to stem the violence, dozens of Sikh demonstrators stormed the parliament of Pakistan in 2014, calling for better protection for their religious sites.

Ramesh Singh, the head of the Pakistan Sikh Council, said the situation has been so alarming that some Sikhs are even afraid of going to the gurdwara, and many of their religious sites have been closed due to the poor security situation. But he added that things have improved since the launch of military operations against militants.

Philippines

Joe Torres

It was past two in the afternoon of September 18, 2015 when bus 1641 of the D'Biel Transit Company arrived and unloaded passengers at the station in the southern Philippine city of Zamboanga. It was a normal Friday afternoon. Farmers were bringing their produce to the city's weekend market, while students from the city's colleges were preparing to board buses to take them home for the weekend. Suddenly there was a loud explosion from inside the bus. Police investigators later said the bomb was placed in the mid-section of the vehicle.

The blast shattered windows, tore off the roof of the vehicle, and killed a teenage student. At least 33 others, including a one-year-old child, were wounded. The explosion paralysed business establishments in some parts of the city.

There were no immediate suspects, but the police said they were looking at the Islamist Abu Sayyaf terror group, which is known for bombing civilian targets and beheading kidnap victims in Mindanao.

Days after the explosion, authorities released a sketch of a male suspect that was labeled 'Muslim type.' The sketch went viral on social media and sparked uproar among Muslims around the country.

Muslims, who comprise between 5and 9percent of the Philippine population, and are the most significant minority in the country, took to Facebook and Twitter to update their profile pictures with the statement, 'I am a 'Muslim type' and I am not a bomber.'

The Young Moro Professionals Network called on Muslims to 'stand and stay united against any form of racism and discrimination.'

'Not all Muslims are terrorists. Some are. Not all Christians are terrorists,' the group said in a statement, adding that 'racial profiling happens not just in the south but in most areas in the Philippines.'

From discrimination to religious persecution

The history of the Bangsamoro, or Moro—the Islamic people of the southern Philippine region of Mindanao—is a history of discrimination and persecution.

Sitti Djalia Hataman, a Muslim princess of the Yakan tribe in the island province of Basilan, admitted that there seems to be 'no persecution on the surface,' but incidents like the bus bombing in Zamboanga 'trigger persecution.'

'Sometimes Filipinos are not aware that they discriminate against others,' said Hataman, who heads the Children of Mindanao Party in the Philippine Congress.

She cited an incident in the House of Representatives after she delivered a speech. 'A colleague asked me where I'd studied. When I said I'd studied in Basilan, the person said, 'No it cannot be, you're so articulate.' Sometimes they tell me that I don't have a Muslim accent or I don't look like a Muslim.'

She said discrimination leads to religious persecution. 'It is religious persecution because of our religious identity as Muslims, even if it has nothing to do specifically about Islam.'

A 2008 study by the US Department of State noted that ethnic, religious and cultural discrimination against Muslim minorities contributed to persistent conflict in the Philippines. The report said that despite religious freedom in the Philippines, Muslims still complain 'that the government has not made sufficient efforts to promote their economic development.'

Some Muslim religious leaders continue to assert that Muslims suffer from economic discrimination by members of the Christian majority in the country. The report said that historically, Muslims have been alienated socially from the Christian majority, and some ethnic and cultural discrimination against Muslims has been recorded.

Roots of the conflict in Mindanao

Teresita Quintos Deles, the Philippine government's adviser on the peace process with Islamist rebel groups in the country, said the 'long drawn-out and vicious conflict' in Mindanao 'involves by and large, Muslims on one side and Christians on the other side.'

However, she emphasised that the conflict is not strictly a religious. She cited 'fault lines' that prevent Moros and Christians coming to an understanding and common cause. Among these fault lines are 'them versus us' and 'north versus south' world views.

"Them versus us' bespeaks of a deep-seated dualism cemented by culture and history,' Deles said, adding that it relates to the Crusades waged against Muslims to reclaim the Holy Land in the Middle Ages.

'When the Spaniards came to the Philippines, Moors would be transmuted into the Moros of the south. Spanish colonial Catholicism then painted Muslims as the heathen, the infidel,' said Deles.

This 'dualism' resurfaced in the wake of the killing of at least 40 police commandos in a bungled raid on a terrorist hideout in Mindanao in January 2015.

Deles noted that phrases like 'Muslims are traitors' and 'Moros cannot be trusted' were uttered even during the ensuing investigation into the incident.

In an address before graduates of the Jesuit-run Xavier University in Cagayan de Oro City, Deles said the 'dualism' in the Filipinos' world view is a result of the 'divide and conquer' strategy of the Spanish and American colonisers 'who pitted us Filipinos in a 'north versus south' contest.'

Religious persecution in the Philippines

Religious persecution in the Philippines should not be understood in terms of martyrdom, a concept that is being used by Islamists in Syria, Lebanon and in other parts of the Middle East, said Doctor Jayeel Serrano Cornelio, director of the Development Studies Program of the Jesuit Ateneo de Manila University. 'We don't have that,' he said.

Cornelio, a sociologist, said there might be anecdotal situations in the Muslim regions of Mindanao, but persecution in the Philippines has to be understood as a 'majority-minority dynamic.' Muslims and other minority religions feel that they are persecuted by the state, which is Catholic, when it comes to economic and political policies.

A 2005 survey by independent pollster Pulse Asia showed that 55 percent of respondents think that Muslims 'are more prone to run amok,' while 47 percent think that they are terrorists or extremists. The study concluded that 'a considerable percentage of Filipinos (33 percent to 39 percent) are biased against Muslims.'

'In social media we see that the Filipino Muslims are really attacked by the majority, which is Catholic,' said Cornelio.

Verbal persecution and persecution in terms of stereotypes are predominant, he said, adding that Muslims feel they are persecuted by the majority's perception that Muslims are poor, or that they are violent because of the conflict in Mindanao.

Cornelio said there is persecution in terms of class position, where a systematic perception prevails that a Filipino Muslim lives in a poor economic situation.

He said Muslims in the Philippines encounter persecution in terms of housing, employment, social protection and even dietary norms. 'It is difficult for Muslims to eat in the Philippines, where halal food is rare,' said Cornelio.

'We have taken for granted that the Philippine public space is Catholic, and it becomes dangerous to be non-Catholic,' he said.

Cornelio said the resistance of the Bangsamoro people in Mindanao is an example of a Manila-centric middle-class persecution, 'a persecution that does not understand the realities in the south.'

Cornelio defined persecution as the 'systematic marginalisation of 'the other' just because he or she does not resonate with your own world view or your own characteristics.' He said religious persecution in the Philippines is a result of the failure of the majority Christians to recognise that Catholicism actually permeates Philippine culture, its politics, the legal system and family life.

It was far from the reality before the arrival of Spanish colonisers, who brought Catholicism to the Philippines in the 1500s, when there were only indigenous beliefs.

'In fact there was no Filipino religion. There were religions and spirituality all over the place, there were different world views, but there was no consciousness of a Filipino society or nation,' said Cornelio.

There could not be discrimination based on religion in that milieu, and if ever there was, it was based on ethnic conflicts, or territorial disputes tied to identity and power.

'Persecution only happens when you have a majority that is dominant,' said Cornelio.

An ethnic conflict, like slave raiding, can also be viewed as persecution, because one tribe sees itself as superior to another, but it is influenced by factors other than religion.

He said that in Philippine society, religion is not usually the basis of violence. 'Religion becomes violent when it becomes the language through which people articulate their feelings of exclusion,' Cornelio said.

In the context of the ongoing conflict in the southern Philippines, religion has been used as a world view to explain violence and therefore persecute other people.

'When you exclude a community, then you're creating a minority, and that minority will solidify their identity, and that can turn violent if push comes to shove, and religion becomes the language to express that exclusion and violence,' Cornelio explained.

He warned that while religion can be a language to express feelings of being persecuted, it can also become a language to express a violent reaction, like what has been happening in Mindanao, especially over the past 50 years.

Islam in the Philippines

Islam is said to have begun taking root in the Philippines around1380, although some scholars believe that it spread in some areas of the archipelago during the early 1200s. The inhabitants of the island of Sulu in the southernmost part of the country have been described as among the earliest converts to Islam. Historians, however, say the converts retained many of their pre-Islamic beliefs because the conversions were mostly done not by full-time religious teachers, but by Arab-Muslim traders.

The Sulu Sultanate was established in about 1450, and Muslim influence spread northward, reaching the island of Luzon. The sultanate was already 71 years old when the Spanish colonisers invaded Moro territories in 1521. The Moros resisted the Spanish colonial policy of subjugation and Christianisation, and by the early 1700s the Sultan of Sulu had defeated the Sultan of Maguindanao, signaling the rise of the Sulu sultanate in Mindanao and the spread of Islam. The Spanish made several attempts to control Jolo, the capital of Sulu, but failed.

Conversion to Islam peaked in the 1970s, at the height of the Moro uprising against the Philippine government. Fearing for their lives, many Christian settlers in Mindanao converted to Islam.

'It was this strong feeling of insecurity that made them decide to convert,' said Dr. Luis Lacar in his unpublished study 'Balik-Islam: Christian Converts to Islam in the Philippines.'

Lacar, who teaches at the Mindanao State University-Iligan Institute of Technology, said that the converts, finding security in their newfound religion, became zealous defenders of Islam. They 'tend to identify more with their newfound faith'—so much so that born Muslims even think 'the converts are overdoing it.'

The most significant factor in bringing about such zeal among the converts is the *dawah* (propagation of Islam), especially by the Tabligh, a missionary movement in Mindanao. The Tabligh became influential in the Philippines during the 1980s, when foreign preachers, especially from Pakistan, Libya and Egypt, arrived in the country. 'It was inevitable,' wrote Lacar, 'that some of the missionaries taught radical Islam.'

The number of Filipino workers who went to the Middle East in the 1980s boosted the ranks of the new Muslims. These Filipinos became Muslims for practical reasons while working in the region as laborers. Having the same faith as their employers was apparently regarded as a plus, and enabled them to enjoy benefits denied other workers, such as being able to stay on and look for other jobs once their contracts had ended. But indications are that many of the converts took their new faith to heart.

In the 1990s, groups propagating the Islamic faith multiplied, some of them composed mostly of converts. Among the more prominent organisations are the Fi Sabilillah Dawah and Media Foundation, the Islamic Studies for Call and Guidance, the Islamic Information Center, and the Islamic Wisdom Worldwide.

Islamic revivalism

Starting in the late 1980s, many young Muslims in the southern Philippines have turned to religion as the 'cure-all' for their disenchantment with the politics served up by the government, and even by separatist Islamist rebels.

The failure of politics to give clear direction to Mindanao society has contributed to the resurgence of Islamic movements in Muslim areas, said Oblates Father Eliseo Mercado.

Mercado, who studied Islam at Al Azhar University in Cairo, warned as early as the late 1980s that the emerging movements 'are militant, aggressive and dynamic.' Many members of the then-rising Islamic movements in the country were young people in their late teens to early 20s 'who are restless, frustrated and dissatisfied … so they turn to religion.'

The economic situation in predominantly Muslim provinces in the country fueled feelings among Muslims that they were neglected.

'There is disillusionment and discouragement,' said Ustadz Abdulgani Yusop, the grand mufti in western Mindanao. He blamed 'economic marginalisation' for the rise of Islamic movements, particularly the fundamentalist ones.

Ishmael Mohammad, 21, was typical of the membership of these growing movements. A former activist in the secessionist Moro National Liberation Front, he said the separatist movements were 'all noise without accomplishing anything.'

'In my belief, only the studying and the following of Islam can be the answer to the problems of the Muslims,' Mohammad said.

Mercado noted that the credibility of Islamic movements lies in the fact that 'they are poor like the masses, and they are not involved in the power play in the traditional sense. They have no business interests. Their leaders were uncompromising.'

Mashur Binghablib Jundam, a scholar at the Institute of Islamic Studies of the University of the Philippines, said many of the young zealots were 'martial law Moro babies' who know and honor only one law—the Koran. Jundam said they have been taught that Mindanao is part of the *umma* (the Muslim 'community'), and it must be taken back from the non-believers.

The late Philippine dictator Ferdinand Marcos declared martial law on September 21, 1972, to suppress increasing civil strife, including a

Moro uprising in Mindanao, and the threat of a communist takeover following a series of bombings in Manila.

Phenomenon of Muslim 'reverts'

Mar Amores was already in his late 20s when Islam caught his attention. Born inoa traditional Catholic family in the central Philippines, Amores was enraged by stories in the media about Moro bandits killing Christians in Mindanao. His hatred encouraged him to learn about the Muslim 'enemy.'

'I wanted to discover what kind of people they are,' said Amores. He read history books, and studied all the available material on Muslims and Islam. After two decades of 'discernment,' his hatred of Muslims has turned into 'understanding.' In 1999, Amores decided to change his name to Zulfikar Muamarjalil Amores, and he became a Balik-Islam (Islam returnee).

Muslims believe that people are born into Islam, while converts are 'reverting' to their original faith. They are thus called 'Balik-Islam.'

'It was a long process,' Amores said. It was a 'cultural liberation' for him, and his concept of God became clear and his view of life and society changed. 'I learned discipline and became free from idols. It's a conversion from vices and sin to humbling oneself before God. It's a personal discovery.'

But it was also a difficult process. 'It's hard to be considered an apostate and live in a society dominated by Christians,' he said. His friends laughed at him and called him 'bandit' and 'Abu Sayyaf.'

'It shows how insensitive the majority of our society is,'said Amores.

Life has become even harder for Balik-Islam like Amores after the reported involvement of Muslim converts in terrorist networks in the country.

Chief Superintendent Rodolfo Mendoza, former intelligence group chief of the Philippine National Police, warned that the new wave of converts to Islam could prove more dangerous than established Muslim guerilla groups.

'Converts are ideal terrorists because they are eager to prove themselves worthy of their new faith,'said Mendoza.

Abdullah Yusuf Abu Bakr Ledesma, former spokesman of the Balik-Islam Unity Congress in the Philippines, claimed that Muslims, especially 'reverts,' are 'under attack.' Ledesma, who used to be called 'Joey' by his friends but now answers to 'Yusuf,' assailed the 'black propaganda' waged by the government and the media against Muslims.

'What we feel as Muslims is different from what comes out in the media,' Ledesma said. He believes many Muslims are filled with a deep 'anti-Western anger' especially as authorities link Islamic groups to terrorist organisations.

'The brotherhood of Islamis under a global attack spearheaded by the United States right now,' said Ledesma, who holds a PhD from the Massachusetts Institute of Technology.

Ledesma said he became a Muslim because Roman Catholicism has been 'hijacked by the West,' and the history of persecutions and dictates by the West 'leaves not a bad taste.'

Islam returnees, though, are nothing new in the Philippines. Even during the Spanish period, some Christians embraced Islam for reasons that ranged from the very personal to the practical. One of the more prominent converts was a Christian fugitive from Cavite named Pedro Cuevas. In 1842, Cuevas escaped to the island of Basilan in Mindanao, where he fought and killed a Muslim chieftain named Datu Kalun. To be recognised leader of the mostly Muslim Yakan natives, Cuevas had to convert to Islam. He adopted the name Datu Kalun, married a Yakan woman, and instituted socio-political changes in the island. Datu Kalun consolidated the natives, led battles against invaders from Jolo, and rid Basilan of pirates and marauders. He died in Basilan on July 16, 1904.

The challenge of fundamentalism

Muslim and Christian partnerships have always been a major concern in the effort to bring peace to the southern Philippines. The situation has been made more complex by the new wave of fundamentalism, both in Islam and in Christianity, in recent years.

'Biases and prejudices are as strong as ever, if not stronger,' noted Oblates priest Eliseo Mercado. He said Filipinos' perception of each other is shaped more by historical memory and the mass media than by actual knowledge and factual experiences.

The rise of fundamentalism, starting in the late 1980s, has become a factor that seems to block Muslim and Christian partnerships in several parts of the country.

'Tragically, secular humankind understands this new religious awakening in a very narrow sense,' said Mercado, adding that various religious revivalist movements in Islam and Christianity, and in other religious traditions, are often, lumped together under a generic label of 'religious fanaticism.'

'Often, this religious 'strain' is interpreted as a reaction to current secular realities. The religious revivalist movement is much wider and broader,' he added.

Many Muslims, like their Christian counterparts, do not accept the label of fundamentalism to describe the current religious 're-awakening.'

Mercado explained that, as in the Christian 're-awakening' movement, the Islamic counterpart represents a desire and a determination to 'return' to the perceived 'basics' or 'fundamentals' of the religious tradition. There are those who attempt to recapture the dynamism of religion and reconcile it with the exigencies of a modern, technological era, and the condition of globalisation, in which old rule cannot possibly remain unaltered.

'Then there are those who embrace the new wave of religious re-awakening, to oppose the increasing secularising trends of contemporary society,' observed Mercado, adding that today there is a strong belief that the surge of religious revivalism is the single factor that erodes inter-religious dialogue and collaboration that have gained currency in the post-Vatican II era.

'Religious re-awakening both in Islam and Christianity, as in other religions, has taken an 'exclusivist' form that views all others as foreign bodies and source of contamination and defilement,' noted Mercado.

Unfortunately, the new religious revivalism is bringing to the fore lingering resentment about injustices in past relationships. Mercado described it as 'a sort of exclusivity of culture and identity, drawing all things into a calculated 'otherness' and reciprocity.'

Addressing persecution

'People are easily misled because of social injustice, poverty and lack of access to education,' said Mussolini Lidasan of the Al Qalam Institute of Islamic Studies at the Jesuit-run Ateneo de Davao University.

'It is not that Christians hate Muslims; it is because both the Filipino Christians and the Muslims lack the opportunity to interact with one another,' Lidasan said. 'It is a complex situation.'

Sociologist Jayeel Serrano Cornelio is optimistic that the proposed establishment of an autonomous region for Filipino Muslims in Mindanao is an opportunity for people to recognise 'the other' in Philippine society.

'The Bangsamoro is a litmus test,' he said, adding that Filipinos must take a broad understanding of persecution.

'Violence does not happen overnight. It is bred in an environment of ignorance and a majority that seems not to understand what is happening in the lives of the minority,' said Cornelio.

He said the Philippines is at a critical juncture with the creation of the Bangsamoro autonomous region. 'It does not promise peace, but it offers better access for Muslims to the resources of the state.'

The establishment of the Bangsamoro autonomous Muslim region is part of the peace deal signed by the Philippine government and Moro rebels in 2014, to end a five-decade-old insurgency.

'Unless people recognise that we are a multicultural and multi-ethnic people, there will always be discrimination and persecution... and people will fight against persecution,' said Sitti Djalia Hataman of the Yakan tribe on Basilan Island. Hataman has filed an anti-discrimination bill in the Philippine Congress that will penalise discriminatory acts such refusing—on religious or ethnic grounds— to offer employment, or to provide education, delivery of goods and services or accommodation.

Should the bill be passed into law, several government agencies, including the Commission on Human Rights, will be tasked with 'providing the procedures for resolution, settlement or prosecution of acts of discrimination.'

In a position paper on the proposed bill, the Center for Alternative Legal Services, an alternative law group, said it is 'imperative' to enact a law that is designed to address the 'skewed order of things, toward a system where no one is excluded from the opportunities that civilised society has to offer.'

'Peaceful co-existence among different peoples requires justice and equality,' the group said.

It added that while prejudices and biases on the basis of ethnicity and religious affinity may not be easily and immediately eradicated, 'the Philippines, as a state-party to various international instruments, should mobilise resources to curb acts of discrimination.'

Eliseo Mercado, however, warned that it requires a 'commitment and determination to steadily school our hearts and minds to resist and reject the habit of preferring suspicion to trust, and the instinct to prefer the familiar confrontation to a new relationship of partnership in a world that is in a difficult transition.'

Sources

Interviews

Rep. Sitti Djalia Hataman, member of the Philippine House of Representatives, Anak Mindanao (Children of Mindanao) Party.

Dr. Jayeel Serrano Cornelio, Director, Development Studies Program, Ateneo de Manila University.

Father Eliseo Mercado, OMI, Islamic scholar from Al Azhar University, Cairo

Mussolini S Lidasan, Al Qalam Institute of Islamic Studies, Ateneo de Davao University

Articles

Sentrong Altenatibong Lingap Panligal, Position paper on the Anti-Discrimination Bills

Aisha Nasarruddin, Filipino Muslims' Struggle for Identity and Homeland: The Plight of the Bangsamoro [http://muslimmatters.org/2012/03/13/filipino-muslims-struggle-for-identity-and-homeland/]

Jose Torres Jr., The Troubled Return of the Faithful [http://pcij.org/imag/SpecialReport/balik-islam.html]

Rohingya Muslims

By John Zaw

Mandalay

U Furukre calls how he fled to a mosqueto escape a mob that was attacking Muslim homes near Sittwe, the capital of Myanmar's Rakhine State, in 2012.

Sitting on a small bench in a squalid refugee camp called Dar Paing, where he was eventually forced to re-settle, the 45-year-old, who has eight children, said' We thought that we would be here temporarily, but we have been here for more than three years.'

U Furukhad opened a shop in a market in Sittwe, and traded with Rakhine Buddhists before violence erupted in 2012. 'I lost my property, my business opportunities, and I have stayed in there fugee camp, un employed and with no human rights,' he said.'I am looking forward to returning to our village near Sittwe.'

Systematic abuses against Rohingya

The Myanmar government denies that the Rohingya even exist. They are officially regarded as Bengalis—implying that they are illegal immigrants from neighboring Bangladesh—and discriminatory legislation effectively renders the vast majority of the Rohingya as stateless.

The Rohingya have been subject to systematic abuse by state and non-state actors for decades. When sectarian violence erupted in Rakhine State in 2012, 200 people were killed and more than 140,000 displaced and forced into IDP (internally displaced people) camps, where they live in desperate, insanitary conditions, with almost universal unemployment.

All Rohingya in Myanmar are denied citizenship under a controversial 1982 citizenship law, and they were also excluded from the country's 2014 census, as the authorities do not permit anyone to identify as 'Rohingya.'Consequently, around 1.2 million people in Rakhine State were left out of the official count

In January 2014,at least 40 Rohingya were killed by security forces and residents in the village of Du Chi Yar Tan in Maungdaw Township, Rakhine State– an incident that sparked the United Nations to call for an impartial investigation, according to New York-based Human Rights Watch (HRW) in a 2015 report.

However, the Myanmar government dismissed the report as 'exaggerated' and vehemently denied that the incident had happened.

Following the massacre of the Rohingya, international aid organisation Medicins Sans Frontieres (MSF) was expelled from Rakhine State by the government. MSF had publicly stated that it had treated 22 Rohingya victims after the incident.

The suspension of MSF in February 2014 left thousands of people without primary healthcare until September, when MSF resumed its activities in Rakhine State

In late March 2015, Rakhine nationalists attacked United Nations and non-governmental organisation (NGO) offices, and forced the evacuation of at least 200 foreign and local aid workers. After the attack, the local government formed the Emergency Coordination Committee (ECC) comprised of local officials, community leaders and NGOs, and which mainly scrutinises the NGO aid to Rohingya who are confined to the camps.

Meanwhile, the government's secret Rakhine State Action Plan for long-term development was leaked. It included provisions for the forced relocation of all Rohingya camps—which together house an estimated 130,000 people—to unspecified sites, and a nationality verification process to determine eligibility for citizenship under the discriminatory 1982 Citizenship Law. Those deemed ineligible would be sent to detention camps and face possible deportation according to Human Rights Watch's annual report in 2015.

After the leak of the draft, the government did not implement the plan, as pressure mounted from the United Nations and international community.

Permanent segregation

Ethnic Rakhine nationalists have lobbied the government of Myanmar to deport Rohingya to third countries, as they strongly oppose any plan for integration or citizenship. Aye Nu Sein, vice chairman of the Arakan National Party (ANP)—a hardline Buddhist party in the Rakhine State—said, 'We don't want all the Rohingya put into the Rakhine State, and they must be scrutinised under the citizenship law.'

'There is much concern about the Rakhine community. Both communities living together is not possible, and the international community should not put pressure on this issue,' said PeThan, a lower-house lawmaker from the ANP.

But U Furuk said that the Rohingya have been living side by side with Rakhine Buddhists for many years, so why can't the two peoples co-exist again.

In downtown Sittwe, around 4,000 Rohingya Muslims live in a squalid ghetto in Aung Mingalar ward that has been sealed off with barbed-wire fences and checkpoints and patrolled by security forces. Aung Mingalar is the only place where Buddhist mobs couldn't burn down Muslim homes in Sittwe town in 2012. The place is off-limits to foreigners and journalists, and the Rohingya residents rely on support from local and international NGOs, with no employment opportunities.

'We are in a virtual prison, as we can't leave the area. We have to be accompanied by local police in emergency cases for healthcare,' said Aung Win, a Rohingya community leader.

Disenfranchisement

In February 2015,the Myanmar government revoked the 'white cards' that had granted voting privileges—predominantly to stateless Rohingya Muslims—and set a deadline of May 31 for holders to turn them in, as part of the national citizenship program. The cards had first been issued for the 2010 national elections.

The ruling came after Shwe Maung, a prominent Rohingya lawmaker with the ruling Union Solidarity and Development Party, was barred from running in the planned November 2015 election because his parents were not Myanmar citizens when he was born.

There were around 700,000 white-card holders in Rakhine State, and some 400,000 cards had been handed in as of the May deadline, according to the government.

Meanwhile, dozens of Rohingya Muslims who ran as candidates in the November 2015 election were disqualified by the Union Election Commission, because of 'citizenship issues.'

Ms. Yanghee Lee, the UN special rapporteur for human rights, expressed 'grave concern' about the disenfranchisement of hundreds of thousands of potential voters and the disqualification of Muslim candidates in the run up to the November polls.'Discrimination against ethnic and religious minorities, including the Rohingya in Rakhine State, should be addressed as a matter of priority,' Ms. Lee said in a November 16, 2015 statement.

Idirs, a 38-year-old community leader in Ohn-Taw-Gyi IDP camp near Sittwe, showed a receipt he got after giving his white card back to local authorities.'We are very sorrowful that we didn't get the right to vote in the2015 election, despite the fact that we could vote in the 2010 election,' he said during an interview in the camp, adding that no one had spoken out on behalf of the Rohingya community since the2012 violence

Desperate conditions

Persecution has led to a Rohingya exodus, often via a perilous boat journey to Malaysiaor Thailand. Rohingyamen, women and children attempting to flee Myanmar by boat in early 2014 were killed or severely beaten by human traffickers if their families failed to pay ransoms. They were often kept in hellish, inhuman conditions, according to London-based Amnesty International.

Aid groups speculate that thousands of people will take the perilous journey to Malaysia when the so-called 'sailing season' starts in November each year, and the numbers could grow due to the disenfranchisement in the 2015 elections.

The United Nations has estimated that more than 100,000 people have already made the journey from Rakhine State and Bangladesh, where grinding poverty is the main driver for migration.

Yasmin, a mother of four who stays in Say Thamar Gyi IDP camp near Sittwe, said she knew that it was a risky journey as she tried to leave for Thailand in May 2015 to find her husband, who had left three years earlier.'I will take a perilous boat journey again, as I believe that it's worth dying at sea rather than living in miserable conditions in the camps,' she said.

Fundamentalism emerges

Myanmar has been ruled by a military regime for more than five decades, and for most of that time was a pariah nation. It is a multi-ethnic and multi-religious country, with 135 official ethnic groups. In 2011, a new quasi-civilian government came to power, offering the hope for a liberalised political and economic system, aiming towards what the ruling junta described as 'disciplined democracy.'

Amid newfound freedom of expression and assembly, hardline Buddhist monks have taken the opportunity to step up anti-Rohingya and anti-Muslim rhetoric.

Ashin Wirathu, an outspoken monk from Mandalay, and one of the leaders of the 969 Movement—an alliance of nationalist groups —is accused of fomenting anti-Muslim sentiment that fueled deadly religious violence in Meikhtila, central Myanmar, in 2013 to Lashio, northern Shan State to Mandalay city in 2014.

U Wirathu denies the allegations, or that his speeches in citesectarian violence.

In 2013, senior Buddhist monks organised the Committee for the Protection of Race and Religion, commonly known as Ma Ba Tha, which was a precursor to the 969 Movement.

The 969 Movement has lobbied the government for the introduction of four race and religion laws that opposition parties and international observers have condemned as discriminatory. The clerics argue that Myanmar's Buddhist identity is at risk from a growing but unspecified threat from the Muslim minority, who account for only about 5 percent of the country's 51 million people.

Critics say that the race and religion laws are squarely aimed at the nation's million or so Rohingya. The regulations impose mandatory birth spacing for women; Buddhist women must register their marriage in advance if they wish to marry a man outside their faith; and restrictions on religious conversions have been enshrined in legislation.

U Parmaukkha, a leading monk from Ma Ba Tha, and who is based in Yangon, claims that the laws are not aimed at oppressing minority Muslims, Hindus and Christians, but rather at protecting Buddhists.

'The religious laws are imposed according to the circumstance of the situation, as neighboring countries like Bangladesh, Pakistan and Indonesia are overwhelmed by Muslims, so we really need to prevent this from happening in Myanmar,' said U Parmaukkha.

Myanmar's outspoken Catholic leader, Cardinal Charles Maung Bo, has condemned the religious laws, saying that parliament has been coerced by a fringe group of the religious elite, which only fragment sthe dream of a united Myanmar. Cardinal Bo reiterated that the compassionate teachings of Buddhism are being threatened in Myanmar by 'peddlars of hatred.'

Bigotry and chauvinism against religious and ethnic minorities grows more pervasive, in some cases provoked by religious figures within the Buddhist community, while the government demonstrated little willingness to intervene, investigate properly, or prosecute those responsible for abuses according to the United States Committee on International Religious Freedom in a 2015 report on Myanmar.

The committee continued to recommend in 2015 that Myanmar be designated as a 'country of particular concern' under the International Religious Freedom Act.

Victims of deep-rooted prejudices

The Economist magazine reported in June 2015 that Muslims probably arrived in what was then the independent kingdom of Arakan (now Rakhine) as long ago as the 8th century. They were seafarers and traders from the Middle East, and were joined in the 17th century by tens of thousands of Bengali Muslims captured by the marauding

Arakanese. Some were forced to serve in the Arakan army, others were sold as slaves, and yet more were forced to settle in Arakan.

'Rohingya' simply means 'inhabitant of Rohang,' the early Muslim name for Arakan. The kingdom was eventually conquered by the Burmese in 1785.

At this juncture there was little tension between the Muslims and the Arakanese. That all changed, however, with the British conquest of Arakan in 1825. As Arakan and Burma were administered as part of British India, hundreds of thousands of Bengalis (or 'Chittagonians' as the British called them) flooded into Arakan to work. By 1941, about a third of the population of Akyab (now Sittwe) was recorded as coming from Chittagong or elsewhere in Bengal, according to the report.

This mass immigration boosted the colonial economy, but local Arakanese bitterly resented it. They had no control over it, believing that their jobs and land were being taken over by people whom they still call 'illegal immigrants,' or just (pejoratively) 'Bengalis.' Relations further soured during the Second World War when the retreating British armed some Muslims to fight against the Rakhine, who had largely sided with the Japanese.

Kyaw Hla Aung, Rohingya community leader and former International NGO worker in Thetkaepyin IDP camp near Sittwe, said that his people have been living in Rakhine for generations, and his father was a civil servant, but he himself is now not entitled to be a citizen of Myanmar.'We are discriminated against and denied citizenship [under the controversial 1982 law] and we are voiceless. The country lacks the rule of law, especially in religiously divided Rakhine State.'

A glimmer of hope

Myanmar's opposition leader Aung San SuuKyi, and her National League for Democracy (NLD) won a landslide victory in the November 8, 2015 election, which was the freest poll in a quarter of century. The NLD is now entitled to choose is own presidential candidate and form a new government.

However, Nobel laureate SuuKyi has been criticised by international rights groups as being silent on the plight of the Rohingya.

Despite her silence on the issue, some Rohingya Muslims hope that the new NLD-led government will be able to restore their rights and improve conditions and the rule of law in divided Rakhine State.

'We hope that the NLD government will be able to restore the rights of Rohingya,' said Hla Win from Ohn Taw Gyi IDP camp, who fled Pauktaw township due to the violence in 2012.

The NLD, however, insists that there are no Rohingya, and that historically the people who came from neighboring Bangladesh are 'Bengalis.'

'It is too early to say publicly what the NLD's plan will be for Muslims in Rakhine State, as they prioritise national reconciliation, peace and economic development,' said Win Htein, a close aide to SuuKyi.

On November 18, 2015, the UN General Assembly's Human Rights Committee criticised Myanmar's treatment of the Rohingya, and called for a change to the citizenship rules to enable Rohingya to become full citizens. The non-binding resolution of a meeting of the 193-nation assembly's third committee 'calls upon the government of Myanmar to protect the human rights and fundamental freedoms of all individuals, including persons belonging to the Rohingya minority.'

The Rohingya should have full citizenship and enjoy all related rights in Myanmar, the resolution said.

Sri Lanka

Quintus Colombage

Colombo, Sri Lanka

In June 2014, the Venerable Watareka Vijitha Thero was stripped naked and beaten on the outskirts of Colombo. The police later discovered him unconscious on the side of a road. The senior Buddhist monk has also received several threatening telephone calls from Buddhist extremistswho want to silence him as he encourages inter-religious dialogue in Sri Lanka. The monk talks about the need for harmony among Buddhists, Muslims and Christians, and has condemned recent attacks on Muslims and Christians in the island nation. He has been called pro-Muslim and 'Mohomad' Watareka.

Religious freedom in Sri Lanka is slowly dying, and violence against minority religions goes un-investigated. Civil rights activists such as Vijitha Thero and Muslim political activist Asath Sally have been jailed under the Prevention of Terrorism Act, for attempting to organise a demonstration against Buddhist extremism.

Vijitha Therohas been a strong critic of the Bodu Bala Sena (Buddhist Strength Force) (BBS) and other Buddhist hardliners, and has on several occasions been attacked as a result. Although he has made several complaints to the Human Rights Commission and the police over the attacks, he said no action has been taken by officials.

'I condemn recent attacks on Muslims and Christians,' said the monk.'Buddhist extremist groups in Sri Lanka are not following the real philosophy of Buddhism. These groups act like terrorists and spread hate among religions. The roof of my house was renovated by a

Catholic priest, and Muslims have spent money to put up the temple building,' the monk said.'I stand for religious harmony in the country, but the result is many nights spent hiding in the jungles to escape the mobs of radical Buddhist monks. Political elites also benefit from disharmony between religions, especially during elections,' he added.

In Sri Lanka, 70 percent of the population is Buddhist, compared with about 10 percent Muslim and 8percent Christian.

In 2014, the radical Sinhalese Buddhist nationalist organisation aligned itself with Myanmar's controversial 969 Movement—a group of nationalistic organisations—to campaign against Muslims and Christians. Preaching hatred and warning of Muslim invasions, monks from BBS, Sinhala Ravaya, Ravana Balaya and an unknown number of other organisations, have been blamed for attacks on non-Buddhists, including Christian places of worship, mosques and Hindu temples. They have even attacked fellow Buddhists who speak out against growing religious intolerance in the country. The United Nations counted some 88 attacks on Muslims and 55 on Christians in 2014.

There are over 400 evangelical churches in Sri Lanka, but mobs led by radical Buddhist monks have attacked a number of them—even during Sunday service. About 105 such places were attacked in 2014, according to the National Christian Evangelical Alliance (NCEASL), and a there was a high number of attacks against minority Christian churches in 2015.

On September 6, 2015, four Buddhist monks forcibly entered a Christian center in Bandaragama and claimed that the pastor had no permission to conduct church services in the village. The police demanded that the pastor register his place of worship with the Ministry of Religious Affairs in order to continue religious activities. However, the registration of religious places of worship is not a legal requirement in Sri Lanka.

In a previous incident on July 23, 2015,12 Buddhist monks arrived with a mob at the Assemblies of God Church in Beliatta and questioned the pastor about his religious activities. They attempted to obtain a letter stating that the pastor was not operating a place of worship. Later that day, the pastor's residence was stoned, causing damage to his trishaw and his home.

'Many of the mobs who attack prayer centers have been led by Buddhist monks, but no action has been taken by the police,' said Pastor Arulanandan Mendis of the Assemblies of God Church.'Like me, many pastors have been beaten and received threats [with the aim of halting prayer meetings]. Our homes and vehicles have been attacked, and we have even stopped sending our children to school,' Mendis added.

An anti-conversion bill was tabled in the Sri Lankan parliament in 2005, and is currently still pending enactment. Christian leaders and evangelical pastors have campaigned against it, as social analysts warn of growing religious intolerance and extremism across Sri Lanka.

Doctor Jehan Perera, executive director of the National Peace Council of Sri Lanka, and a regular columnist for national newspapers, said that the majority of the people in Sri Lanka are Sinhalese Buddhists, many of whom see themselves as a threatened minority in South Asia, even though they are a majority in Sri Lanka. 'Because of this insecurity, they can be very nationalistic when they feel threatened by those of other religions or ethnicities,' said Perera, who holds a Doctor of Law degree from Harvard Law School.

The Sri Lankan constitution gives the 'foremost place' to Buddhism, and although members of other religions are constitutionally assured of equal treatment, in practice the state favors Buddhism,' said Perera.

According to Perera, governments have tended to defer to clergy of all religions. The Lessons Learnt and Reconciliation Commission (LLRC), appointed in 2011 by the previous government, noted that the core values of the four main religions practiced in Sri Lanka— Buddhism, Hinduism, Islam and Christianity—enable a basis on which reconciliation can be constructed.

The 30-year civil war in Sri Lanka—waged between Tamil separatists and government forces, and which claimed tens of thousands of lives—ended on May 19,2009. The former government then established the LLRC to work together to find a political solution to bring permanent peace to the country.

'The present government's proposal of a 'Compassion Council' becomes particularly relevant in this regard. Religious leaders such as the prominent Buddhist monk, the Venerable Maduluwave Sobitha Thero, have become a bridge in the post-war years,' Perera said.

In its latest annual rights report, Britain's Foreign and Commonwealth Office pointed out a high number of incidents targeting minority Christian and Muslim communities in Sri Lanka. In a joint UN rights resolution, noted the report, the UK and other nations expressed alarm at the significant surge in such attacks.

The UN Human Rights Commission noted in a 2015 hearing on Sri Lanka in Geneva, that religious intolerance is growing, and it called for greater investigation by authorities.

Buddhist hardliners have made comments against Halal butchers, the wearing of beards by Muslim men, the wearing of traditional head coverings by Muslim women, and the observance of Muslim prayer times. The Sinhala Ravaya group has asked the police to ban Muslim burqas, claiming the traditional female garments are a grave threat to national security. These groups are also calling for strict measures to be enforced regarding anti-conversion to other religions in Sri Lanka.

Sri Lankan rights monitors, international rights monitors and other critics say that the government has turned a blind eye to attacks by the BBS against Muslims, Christians and critics of the BBS.

The BBS and other Sinhala Buddhist hardliners deny any involvement in attacks against churches, mosques and Muslim businesses.'We greatly respect harmony among religions in the country, but Muslim women should remove their veils, as no one can identify whether they are men or women,' said the Venerable Galagoda Aththe Gnanasara Thero, general secretary of the BBS.

'Muslims have their own banking system and try to impose their ritualistic food products like halal butchers,' Gnanasara Thero said.

The former government launched a special police unit in 2014 to address rising tensions between Christians, Muslims and the Buddhist majority, and the new cabinet drafted a bill seeking to ban racist and religious extremist groups during the new government's '100 Days Work Program,' but did not presented it in parliament.

The Venerable Ittekande Saddhatissa Thero, general secretary of Ravana Balaya, has previously warned 20 evangelical churches to halt their activities in majority Buddhist Polonnaruwa. 'We have hundreds of complaints from Buddhists and Hindus that evangelical pastors convert Buddhists into their religion, and offer gifts and money to them,' Saddhatissa Thero said.

Radical Sinhalese Buddhist nationalist organisations contested the election in August 2015but did not win even one seat in parliament. They claimed to have been let down by previous political alliances. They had previously held close ties with the Freedom Party (SLFP) and former president Mahinda Rajapaksa.

Catholic priest, Father Reid Shelton Fernando, chaplain of the Young Christian Workers' movement, and a university lecturer and human rights activist, said that Buddhists, Hindus, Muslims and Christians do live in harmony in Sri Lanka, but some disgruntled religious fanatics—mainly Sinhalese Buddhist nationalist groups— harbor ill feelings and are vengeful, so the future remains uncertain.

'This is a serious threat to social peace and harmony, even though the founders of all religions were very forthright about non-violence. It is a tragic situation,' said Fr. Fernando.

'Diversity of religions should not be taken as a divisive element that causes suspicion among the followers of other religions. This can destroy peace and harmony in the country, if taken negatively. On the contrary, this diversity should be seen as a blessing that will enrich the followers of other living faiths.'

Christians, he said, had developed a very sober attitude by initiating a process of dialogue with other faiths. This began over 50 years with the Second Vatican Ecumenical Council, held from 1962 to 1965 in Rome. The idea was to change attitudes towards other faiths. Instead of claiming that Christianity is the only true religion, they began to assert that there are values of truth and goodness in other religions.

However, Fr. Fernando said that some actions can create ill-will—such as mosques using noisy loudspeaker systems that cause annoyance to others in the community—which can lead to feelings of persecution when complaints are made.

'Religion is a part of society, economics, politics and culture. The key personalities in the major religions have to raise their voice against religious violence and against religious persecution. Religion should not become a tool in the hands of political leaders; it must become an agent of real change in delivering a value system for all of us to be good citizens in society,' the priest said.

The June 2014assault on Watareka Vijitha Therocame a few days after radical Buddhists hurled petrol bombs and looted the houses and businesses of Muslims, killing four and seriously injuring more than 150 others, during clashes between Buddhists and Muslims in two majority-Muslim coastal towns. A group of individuals later obstructed a press conference in Colombo, and Vijitha Thero was verbally abused by the BBS general secretary Gnanasara, in front of the media.

Jehan Perera said there is evidence that the Buddhist fundamentalists who have come to prominence in the last few years are supported by sections of the previous government.

At the same time, there is concern that Muslim fundamentalism is growing, due to Saudi Arabian support for the Wahabibranch of Islam. Some Sri Lankans are also known to have joined Islamic State in Syria (ISIS), Perera said.

'Christian fundamentalists who are supported by Church groups in the United States are also a concern, as they try to convert those of other faiths, which causes much resentment. However, the fact is that the number of Christians in Sri Lanka, as a percentage of the population, has been steadily falling over the past few decades, due to emigration,' Perera said.

In general, Perera added, the government does not wish to get involved in formally prosecuting religious clergy who have been violent. This is not only in regard to radical Buddhists—although they are the most visible and numerous in terms of offenses against other religions.

According to Fr Fernando, the very victims of religious persecution, by their negative closed mentality, without openness to others, create suspicion among others. It is they who invite would-be perpetrators to act. Sometimes the minorities, through their non-resilient attitude, create an opportunity for extremists who are waiting to act violently.

The right to freedom of religion is a basic right that needs to be proclaimed, the priest said. 'Each religion will have to play a major role in creating harmony between the followers of all religions. It is the task of religious leaders to proclaim that their beliefs may permeate society and all aspects of human life. Economics, politics and culture must be enhanced by a value system from all religions.'

Vietnam

By ucanews.com reporter

Once a year, Maria* accompanies her parish priest and a small delegation of parishioners to Vietnam's Central Highlands to distribute food and clothes, hold religious activities and meet with struggling fellow Christians. It's a mission the 61-year-old has been carrying out since she was a child, and one that never fails to move her.

In Ho Chi Minh City, the group rises at dawn for the day-long trip into Vietnam's remote mountainous region. 'I love the ethnic people and I really feel sorry for them because up there, they are under a lot of pressure from the government,' she said.

In a nation where repression is the norm, Vietnam's Christian and Catholic indigenous minorities have faced particular hardship. Churches have been razed and practitioners blocked from attending services. Visiting pastors are routinely harassed and detained.

'In the past, the local government wouldn't let us gather in a group and wouldn't let us attend our house church. There used to be one there, but after 1975, the government took it and turned it into a community center,' recalls Dinh, an evangelical Protestant who grew up in Quang Ngai Province in central Vietnam. For decades, local authorities refused to return the property, and it wasn't until 2009 that they returned the land and allowed the house church to be rebuilt.

Those practicing unregistered versions of Christianity, however, have fared even worse. In a comprehensive report issued by the New York-based Human Rights Watch (HRW) in 2015, the group highlighted violent, systemic oppression of those practicing De Ga

Protestantism and Ha Mon Catholicism—two sects not recognised by the government.

'I was hit everywhere; they even used electricity to shock me, so I would answer their questions. The police hit me with their hands on both sides of the face. After they hit me, I couldn't hear anything,' a Montagnard Christian told HRW. 'The police told me if I continued going to church, then they would continue arresting me. I was afraid that I would get into trouble with the police again, so that is why I left Vietnam.'

Open Doors, a Christian non-governmental organisation (NGO) that monitors persecution, has ranked Vietnam as one of the worst countries to be Christian on its World Watch List. The country is ranked 16 among 50, and the group describes incidents of 'severe persecution.'

'Search and hunt' activities carried out by the government have sent hundreds of Montagnards fleeing to seek asylum. Most of them have ended up in Cambodia, where they have been sheltered in neighboring highland provinces by Cambodians of the same hill tribe minority. But under pressure from Hanoi, the Cambodian government has had little compunction about making arrests and deportations. A handful of Montagnards have been given refugee status, but far more have been labeled 'economic migrants' and repatriated.

Sister Denise Coughlan, director of the Jesuit Refugee Service in Cambodia, said, 'The government should process them all, but some will not get refugee status.' For those deserving of refugee status but are refused, 'safety is my major concern, and we are trying for room to negotiate for those most in need of protection.'

In 2014, 13 Montagnards were granted refugee status, but more than 200 others saw their applications denied. Many have simply been pushed back across the border, an illegal process known as refoulement. Back in Vietnam, their prospects are bleak. Amnesty International notes that at least one deported asylum seeker was beaten by the police when he returned, while more than 30 were detained overnight.

Such incidents are far from isolated. Region, ethnicity, religion and political activity all play a major role in the authorities' responses. But, as the UK noted in its last report on religion in Vietnam, 'Ethnic minority Protestants continue to experience some of the harshest treatment by local authorities.'

Unchecked expansion

In spite of explicit and implicit pressures, religions have been flourishing in Vietnam—perhaps none more so than Christianity, and Catholicism in particular. Evangelical Protestantism has also experienced growth. The government's own census shows an increase from 410,000 adherents in 1999 to 734,000 adherents a decade later. Today, the government puts that figure at around 1 million, while Church officials insist it is closer to 2 million. Churches themselves report booming membership, with Sunday services often spilling out the doors as new worshipers crowd in.

Despite the best efforts of the authorities, the spread Christianity among ethnic minorities has been particularly rapid. While reliable statistics do not exist, the U.S. State Department wrote in its last religious freedom report that 'based on adherents' estimates, two-thirds of Protestants were members of ethnic minorities.'

'Vietnam has many ethnic minorities, and they become Christian much more quickly than the Kinh [majority],' said Anh,* who helps her pastor husband run a small evangelical Protestant house church in Ho Chi Minh City. Hoang,* the pastor, runs frequent missionary trips, and said the growth of Christianity in Vietnam's Central Highlands is hard to overstate.

'The government there is very harsh, and wants to stop them, but they're still growing strongly because God has changed their lives,' he insisted.

That growth has come in spite of major obstacles. While Protestantism is one of the 38 religions officially recognised by the Vietnamese government, its activities are frequently banned outright by local authorities. Most evangelism is considered illegal, and Church members report that their activities are monitored and curtailed. The government has applied pressure to prevent a merger of the northern and southern evangelical Churches, a move aimed at keeping the north (which is more heavily restricted and has not seen the religious growth of the south) in check.

Even in Ho Chi Minh City, which is arguably the most religion-friendly area of Vietnam, pastors report being monitored.

'Once, I was preaching in a nearby area, and the police 'invited me' and lectured me for four hours. They said, 'You can't spread religion,' and I replied, 'People ask, so I answer.' This has happened three times,' recalled Hoang.*

While the situation has generally improved, he said government control remains omnipresent.'There is less threat from the outside now, but from the inside they still want to take action,' he said.

Quang,* who heads the Tan Thuan Evangelical Church in Ho Chi Minh City, said movement is controlled to no small degree.'We're allowed to hold activities according to our registration papers that say, 'in the next year, I want to do this or that.' You have to let the government know in advance, and you can only follow what that paper says.'

A quieter persecution

For Vietnamese Catholics, the situation is slightly better. Unlike in the early days of communist control, the government now tends to stay out of ecclesiastical affairs. While there are cases of officials axing names from ordination lists, even those priests are permitted to quietly serve. And unlike in China, which continues to follow the model of government-appointed bishops, appointments in Vietnam are left in the hands of the Vatican.

The greater difficulty for the Catholic Church today is handling a mercurial and far from monolithic government. What is permissible in some areas may be punished with jail time in others. Authorities who look the other way for years might suddenly decide to crack down without warning.

'By document, religion is free. But in reality, there is control, especially in the rural areas. It's not easy to build a church or do other [basic pastoral] activities,' said a senior Jesuit official, who asked not to be named because open discussion of religion is still sensitive.

Though precise figures are hard to come by, the Catholic population appears to be growing. In 1954, Catholics made up approximately 1.9 million of the roughly 30 million population, according to research published by the Reverend Doctor Peter Hansen, a lecturer at

Australia's Catholic Theological College. Today, there are 6.2 million Catholics—7 percent of the population.

Over the years, as Vietnam has opened up, abuses have become rarer. But they are far from having ended.

In August 2015, two Catholic youth activists were arrested after serving four years in prison for attempting to 'overthrow the government'—the pair was part of a group of at least 17 Christian and Catholic activists arrested and sentenced at around the same time on charges widely considered to be spurious. In 2013, a group of 14 were sentenced to between three and 13 years in prison after holding peaceful protests or calling for freedom of expression.

In November 2015, a Vietnamese Catholic activist under house arrest was assaulted twice by police in two separate incidents. Another was detained for almost a day and allegedly beaten as well. Both are Redemptorists who have served lengthy jail sentences for outspoken criticism of government policies.

Phil Robertson, deputy director of the Asia Division of Human Rights Watch, said the attacks and arrests are 'part of a daily cycle of systematic and pervasive rights abuses occurring across Vietnam, where an order to target a dissident comes down from the Ministry of Public Security, and the police act like the attack dogs they are— arresting and beating until they are told to stop. All across Vietnam, dissidents are being targeted this way—the only difference is whether the incidents become public or are hushed up.'

Even fairly benign activity is monitored and controlled. Until 2015, a group of interreligious leaders met regularly in a Redemptorist church in Ho Chi Minh City to discuss challenges they faced; now, according to a member, they have to move around after police took exception to the fact that some participants weren't government-approved.

Special targets

The situation in Vietnam may well deteriorate in the coming years. Vietnam's legislature is expected to soon pass a new law on religion and belief that will impose even more monitoring and control of religious activities.

Christian Solidarity Worldwide, and dozens of other international organisations including the International Commission of Jurists and Freedom House, warned in November 2015 that the law in its current iteration will 'act as a powerful instrument of control, placing sweeping, overly broad limitations on the practice of religion or belief within Vietnam, perpetuating the already repressive situation.'

The law is likely to impose especially harsh controls on unregistered or splinter sects that the government so fears.

'To the outside world, Vietnam allows the freedom to follow any religion, but it's not true. The government wants to toughen the law – it's like tightening the noose,' said Le Quang Hien, a HoaHao Buddhist leader in Ho Chi Minh City and member of the Interfaith Council of Vietnam.

Hien, who practices an independent form of HoaHao, has faced particular challenges from the authorities. His office has been taken and his activities monitored. In a landmark evaluation published in 2014 by the UN special rapporteur, Heiner Bielefeldt, on freedom of religion and belief, independent practitioners such as Hien are reported to face a particular threat.

'Independent communities of HoaHao Buddhism, who have engaged in peaceful forms of protest, such as hunger strikes, have been harshly punished, including with repeated or long-term imprisonment. Security agents and hired thugs have reportedly not hesitated to use excessive force during arrests or attacks on these communities, for organising gatherings to pray at so-called 'illegal minarets' that were built for religious congregation purposes,' writes Bielefeldt.

The treatment echoes that meted out to all independent religions. In addition to the harassment of Christian Montagnards, the government has made similar physical attacks on independent Cao Dai followers, members of a splinter Mennonite church, and those in the unrecognised Unified Buddhist Church of Vietnam.

In his report, Bielefeldtargues that the behavior toward those practicing unregistered religion demonstrates Vietnam's true attitude toward religion.

'Whereas religious life and religious diversity are a reality in Vietnam today, autonomy and the activities of independent religious or belief communities—that is, unrecognised communities—remain restricted and unsafe, with the rights to freedom of religion or belief of these communities grossly violated in the face of constant surveillance, intimidation, harassment and persecution,' he writes.

Across Vietnam, meanwhile, everyone is feeling the heat. Maria, the Catholic devotee from Ho Chi Minh City, bemoans the shrinking space for religious freedom in spite of great sacrifices made over the decades.

'During the [independence] war, many people died for their religion. To make a change for Vietnam, many sacrificed themselves,' she said. 'But from my point of view, if the government puts pressure on Catholics, it's because God wants it that way. God wants to train Catholics to be strong.'

Names have been changed, or nicknames used, at the request of interviewees concerned for their security.

CPSIA information can be obtained
at www.ICGtesting.com
Printed in the USA
FFOW02n1004010417
33967FF